the
no-spend
challenge
GUIDE

How to stop spending money
impulsively, pay off debt fast, and
make your finances fit your dreams

JEN SMITH

Printed in the United States of America
First Printing, 2017
Second Edition, 2021

ISBN 978-1979464604

www.ModernFrugality.com

Your Free Gift

As a small token of thanks, I'd like to give you a special bonus to help you get through this book, and reach your financial goals, faster. I've created a 40-page digital workbook that includes (almost) everything you'll need to be successful with a 30-day No-Spend Challenge including:

- Guided prompts for each step laid out in the book
- Day-by-day activity, decluttering, and side hustle recommendations
- Five unique no-spend trackers
- 30 one-sentence journaling prompts
- 52 free activities
- And more!

No-Spend Challenges aren't easy, you can have all the information in the world but what success comes down to is saying "yes" to the small things every single day.

Get your code to download the 30-Day No-Spend Challenge Workbook for free at www.modernfrugality.com/challengeguidegift

And you can find links to every resource and recommendation in this book at www.modernfrugality.com/recommendations-from-the-no-spend-challenge-guide

Dedication

Forever and always, to Travis and Kai.
You still brighten my days and drive my work. I love you.

Contents

Foreword

In 2012, my husband and I both landed what we considered to be our dream jobs—professional positions as managers in cubicles under artificial lights. We thought we'd made it. But a strange thing happened. We found ourselves working for the weekends and counting down the hours to 5 pm every single day. Despite working so hard for these jobs, neither of us felt true passion for what we did on a daily basis.

While we looked like we'd made it—living in the heart of Cambridge, attending yoga, going out to dinner every week— we weren't fulfilled. Our deepest contentment came from our weekend trips hiking. We asked ourselves the question: why are we living in the city, working jobs we don't like so we can "escape" every Saturday to a life we want to live? A simpler life with less clutter, less busyness, more nature.

That question catapulted us into navigating our way out of the "American Dream" and its attendant cycle of consumerism and materialism, and into a life we didn't have to escape from. A life we designed intentionally instead of situationally. I started my blog, Frugalwoods.com, in 2014 to document this journey and my book Meet the Frugalwoods was published in 2018.

Since there weren't many folks in my life who shared my views, I built an online community of like-minded people who value living life above spending money. The idea resonated and I've built my blog to a community of over 100,000 frugal folks. Jen is one of those people.

I met Jen at a conference in 2017, shortly before she published the first edition of The No-Spend Challenge Guide. She'd been a Frugalwoods reader for about a year, during which time she and her husband were working to pay off $78,000 of debt. She started writing about her experience on her blog and was just getting started writing for larger personal finance websites. It was evident she was determined to do more than write on the internet. She wanted to help people change their lives by achieving financial freedom.

Since then, she's published three books, grown the #1 frugal living podcast on Apple Podcasts, and fulfilled her goal of helping people in their pursuit of financial freedom.

I've had the pleasure of being a guest on the Frugal Friends Podcast several times and speaking at their annual frugal living summit, The Future of Frugal. Every time I sit down with Jen and her co-host Jill, we explore topics of frugality and mindful spending that most gurus bury under hotter subjects like crypto.

Jen speaks from true experience—paying off $78,000 of debt is no easy feat! She knows what it's like to say no to things you want in pursuit of long-term goals. You'll never hear her patronize anyone and when you read her book or listen to her show, she makes you feel like you're in the same room, chatting over coffee about how to align your spending with your values.

Jen focuses on the deeper issues behind overconsumption and encourages people to not just practice frugality as a way to get out of debt or retire early, but as the solution to larger issues in our lives.

Excessive consumption has been ingrained in our brains as the solution to our problems. In reality, it keeps people from financial security and builds kingdoms of clutter in our houses, schedules, bank statements, and environment.

Recent studies have shown that 80% of the world's natural resources are used by only 20% of the world's population. And while Americans represent only 5% of the population, we consume 15% of the world's gross domestic product. Even though we buy many of our clothes and products from factories abroad, we're still leading producers of greenhouse gasses and waste.

When considering a problem as big as climate change (or personal finance), it's tempting to throw your hands up in defeat. There's no way one person can make a dent, right? But Jen is a true believer that the fight isn't unwinnable and that every action counts. I also love how she isn't an extremist—she simply shows you how to buy less of what doesn't matter so you can afford more of what does. She teaches a lifestyle that focuses on fulfillment as opposed to materialism.

Every week on the Frugal Friends Podcast, I hear stories of listeners who've paid off debt, saved money, or increased their retirement savings because of tips and wisdom that Jen and Jill share. They're solving the problem of overconsumption one episode at a time and this book is an extension of that mission.

In this book, you'll not only find a guide on how to structure a no-spend challenge but strategies for sticking with this lifestyle change and getting the most from it long term.

If you're ready to overcome impulsive spending and reach your financial goals faster, a no-spend challenge is a great way to start. I can say with sincerity that you're in good hands with Jen.

—Elizabeth Willard Thames, aka Mrs. Frugalwoods
Author of *Meet the Frugalwoods: Achieving Financial Independence Through Simple Living*

Introduction to
The Second Edition

When I wrote the original edition of The No-Spend Challenge Guide I was 28 years old. The feeling of accomplishment from paying off $78,000 of debt in two years was fresh in my mind, as was the difficulty that came with it.

Now, it's the end of 2021.

Not only am I different—now in my thirties, with a child, running a successful financial literacy business—but it also seems like the whole world has changed too. Some of the recommendations that made sense in 2017 aren't so simple now. Some things I took for granted then aren't as easy as I once thought.

We've all aged a decade since 2020, so this book was in need of an update. I dug into the reviews that offered constructive criticism and expounded on research for which I wanted to give more actionable guidance. Everything updated in this book is meant to give you better support to take action. Because I still believe personal finance (as with anything we succeed with) is 20% knowledge and 80% action.

But some things didn't change. I've tried to preserve as much of the headspace I was in when I wrote the original edition, because no one understands what it's like to pay off debt more than someone who just finished paying off their debt. The further someone gets away from a struggle the less they remember what it was like to feel the pain of going through it. And the less pain we remember, the harder it is to empathize with others who experience it later.

My goal was to combine the original feel of the book with the perspective I've gained in the last four years. Since writing the original edition I've been writing and researching personal finance topics almost daily, and I've gained a new perspective living "life after consumer debt." I'll give you a spoiler: Becoming debt-free was not the answer to all my money problems! But I still credit it with the catalyst that led to my life transforming for the better.

I love this book. Reading the reviews, messages on Instagram, and emails about how this book has changed people's perspectives on personal finance has given me so much joy. I don't feel like I deserve it, but I cherish it.

So I hope I gave this guide the updates it deserves so that you can benefit from the magic of No-Spend Challenges: a simple concept, but a powerful tool for self-discovery and financial growth.

Introduction

My first No-Spend Challenge came out of necessity. I was in college and I had $7 in my bank account to last until my next paycheck.

I revisited the challenge when I used up the last of my stipend while working at a nonprofit.

And again as I worked to pay off my student loans.

A lot of people thought my husband and I were crazy for giving up so much to pay off our debt. But our dream wasn't to be debt-free for the sake of saying we're debt-free.

It's just the first step to realizing our dream of financial freedom: The freedom to live without relying on a weekly paycheck.

But a lot of people think financial freedom is a luxury reserved for upper-middle-class white people and crazy entrepreneurs on Shark Tank. (#squattypotty)

Living without worrying about money isn't a fantasy. But for those of us who know how it feels to look tens of thousands of dollars of debt in the face, it can seem like it.

Debt is one of the biggest problems facing our generation. A toxic combination of student loans, credit cards, car loans, and more keep us tied down to jobs we dislike, stuck in apartment leases we can't break, and mentally weighed down by shame we can't escape.

We ignore our debt while it compounds and increases because it's easier to ignore it than to deal with the anxiety it causes. Meanwhile, we spend money to mask the discomfort. Sometimes it's on stuff, but since that's become taboo we spend on experiences, or our children, justifying it as more fulfilling. **Regardless of where it goes, spending every penny of our paycheck (and then some) has become so common people think they can't live any other way.**

I watch so many of my friends blow money on things they don't need or want. I assumed I noticed it while paying off debt due to a ~~little~~ lot of jealousy, but I still see it. I go to houses with fridges and pantries stuffed with grocery store impulse buys. I shop at thrift stores packed with clothes that still have tags on them. All the while knowing much of it will end up in a landfill, contributing to our country's expensive waste problem.

And when we *do* finally become aware and try to change, it's a rude awakening to how ingrained our spending habits are. We want to achieve big dreams like paying off debt, buying a house, retiring early, or traveling abroad, but the habits of impulsive and thoughtless spending make it hard to make ends meet, let alone get ahead.

It's not all on the consumer. It's a wonder anyone can keep money in their pockets. When's the last time you went five minutes without hearing a commercial for this, seeing an ad for that, or getting an email about another "semi-annual sale?"

It's hard out there for anyone with financial goals.

Why Should I Care Now?

Unlike a mortgage, on which interest compounds monthly, student loan interest compounds *daily*. On a 10-year repayment plan, a $37,000 student loan at 4.45% accrues $4.51 in interest every single day. Meaning you'll pay almost $9,000 more than you took out. If you're on a 20-year repayment plan, you end up paying about $19,000 more than you borrowed.

Is not prioritizing your debt worth $19,000?

And that's a pretty conservative figure. I know a lot of people with six figures of student loan debt and interest rates north of 6.5%.

If you don't have student loan debt, maybe you have a car payment. At the time of writing this, auto loans are running anywhere from 4% to 20% depending on your credit score. The average interest rate for a used car is 8.66%, which adds about $5,000 to a $25,000 loan over 60 months.

The cost is similar for a new car. The average rate and price for a new car are 4.09% and $41,000 respectively, which again adds about $5,000 to your total cost.

Imagine setting $5,000 on fire to drive a car with a few more tech options.

But people aren't taught to think about the total cost. We're taught to enjoy the things we can finance and struggle with the things we can't. It's that cycle that keeps us entrenched in debt and paycheck-to-paycheck living.

Eliminating consumer debt gives you the freedom to earn and spend the way you want. And it gives you the freedom to explore what it is you actually want.

If you ever want to experience that freedom, you need to start getting your finances under control *now*. Every day you wait, more of your money belongs to big banks and bad spending habits are drilled deeper into your psyche, padding the pockets of big corporations.

A well-known Chinese proverb says, "The best time to plant a tree was 20 years ago. The second best time is now." You can do this no matter how big your debt is, but the longer you wait, the harder it's going to be.

Now is the time to do the hard work of confronting your debt, savings, and investments. And for many, the first step to financial freedom will be paying off debt.

I think of paying off debt like climbing a mountain. A mountain always looks impossible to climb when you're standing at the bottom. From far away it seems like a good idea, but once you get to the base, which is the best place to start, the idea suddenly becomes unachievable. If you choose to climb the mountain, the journey is hard, but others have done it and the path is clearly carved along the way. And once you're over the summit, you're never the same.

It becomes part of your story, your identity. And after some time you look back on the struggle with fondness. Because not only did you get to the other side, which was the goal when you started; your journey gave you so much more. Perseverance, patience, self-discipline, and lessons you can pass on to others who want to climb the same mountain.

It may not be pretty, but I've talked to hundreds of people who've climbed their mountains and are grateful for their journeys. It takes time, but it's worth the pain.

Start now and not only will you pay less in interest and forfeit less of your hard-earned money to skilled marketers, but you'll also discover how to align your life with your most important values. And that's the ultimate definition of financial freedom.

The road is hard but the destination is reachable. And the techniques I'm sharing in this book will help you reach it faster.

So start now. Challenge yourself to take the first step. Because once you take the first step, the second and third steps become much easier. And I may be a little biased, but I think a no-spend challenge is a great first step.

Who Am I?

I ignored my debt for years, paid as little as $26 per month to my $50,000 student loan, and fell off the budget wagon more times than I'd like to admit. I've even suffered anxiety attacks thinking about my debt.

I was conditioned from a young age to think spending money is a hobby. While some families camped or went to the beach, every weekend my mom and I would go shopping at the mall or make a trip to Target. I had all the symptoms of a spoiled, over-achiever. Who, because I made good grades at school, thought I knew everything about everything, everywhere.

I was so wrong.

I spent years after graduate school stressed and anxious about my debt. I had more student loan debt than I thought I'd ever be able to make in a year at my socially philanthropic, but low-paying dream job.

But then I met who I assume is the most frugal person in existence, and I married him. One of the first things my husband Travis said once we were engaged was that he wanted to pay off his student loans ASAP.

And I was like, heck no.

I didn't want to waste the best years of my life under a rock while he paid off his debt. I don't know why I assumed fun ended at thirty. I can confidently report that it doesn't.

Even with my stubbornness, I knew in my heart he was right. And once he challenged me to imagine what our life could look like without $1,000 monthly debt payments, I knew it was worth forfeiting "the best years of my life" to make our future easier. So I reluctantly committed to this insane idea that we'd pay off our debt as quickly as possible.

Our debt payoff timeline started as a five-year plan. As we got side jobs and raises and learned to spend less and less, that five-year plan turned into four years, then three, until we realized we could pull this thing off in just two years.

I don't even know how the timeline got so much shorter. The only explanation I can come up with was that I didn't believe in myself enough to plan for a two-year debt repayment. It wasn't until we got started that we learned what we were capable of achieving.

Exactly 23 months after we pulled into the driveway from our honeymoon, we made the final payment on what ended up being almost $78,000 of car and student-loan debt. The whole time, we never made more than $88,000 annually.

In 2017, being "debt-free" didn't feel real and sometimes it still doesn't. I tell people we're "consumer debt-free" because technically we still have a mortgage. I still take for granted what an amazing accomplishment it was. The pain of struggling to make extra debt payments each month and missing out on things to save money doesn't sting as much as it did. What I thought would end me didn't.

I don't consider myself at an advantage to pay off a lot of debt quickly. I wasn't raised with an allowance or taught how to budget and save. My parents had one high school diploma between them and never made a lot of money, so I think they were ashamed to talk about it.

I wasn't able to gain momentum easily either. I didn't have a high-paying job, I couldn't even get full-time hours at the one I had, and Travis was unemployed twice in those first six months.

I also didn't have people in my life whom I could ask for money advice. So much of our success comes from our network and mentors. Early in our lives, it comes from our parent's network and mentors. All the people my family and I knew were as clueless about money as I was.

The only thing I did differently was keep going. Some days were better than others, and sometimes I spent $180 on home décor at Target. But every single day that I tried, I got better at earning more and spending less.

Through trial and error, I learned what I could and couldn't live without. I used to think I should only shop at *this* nice store or buy *these* expensive products. I spent hundreds of dollars each month at restaurants I didn't like and coffee shops I went to out of habit, and I was oblivious to how much it drained my bank account.

Learning how to say "no" to myself and how to live a full life with the things I value changed the game for me. The quest to discover more about what I love—and, maybe more importantly, what I don't—inspired me to do more and more until my expenses were finally a check my income could cash.

Today I consider myself financially free. I'm no millionaire, but I'm free to do work I love and turn down work I don't want to do. I get to host the Frugal Friends Podcast full-time, which is mostly hanging out with one of my closest friends and talking about money as often as possible. I was able to leave 9-to-5 employment when my son was born in 2019, and in 2020 when airlines shut down, Travis was able to take a voluntary three-month leave at half pay.

I've spent almost every working day of the last four years helping people escape the trap of overconsumption to find freedom in frugality, all while creating a full life that any income can support.

And that's what I hope you find: your own full life. It may not look like mine, but once you stop taking the words of gurus as law and start designing your own version of financial freedom, you'll find you enjoy the pursuit of it.

I Promise You

I promise that if you do everything in this book, you will be equipped to pay off your debt and reach your financial goals faster than you ever dreamed possible.

Even if you only take half of the steps outlined in this book, you'll be so much farther ahead than your peers and be on the road to being a financial powerhouse.

The longer you wait to start, the more interest eats away at your paychecks and the less money you'll have for the important things in life. If you want to have the financial security to start a business, stay home with your kids, or travel more, then **you can't wait.**

Be the kind of person who has control of their spending. The kind of person your mom brags about at parties. The kind of person who inspires your friends to be better. The kind of person who does more than talk.

Be the person who takes action.

No-Spend Challenges helped me take control of my spending. These methods have been tested and refined over years. They're not perfect and I don't offer any guarantees. But I did this stuff, and it worked. These tips took me from an anxious overspender to a bonafide conscious consumer.

Each chapter will give you practical insight and tips on breaking habits, help you find alternatives to spending, and show you how to make the most of your time.

If you want to skip right to the practical tips, go to chapter 3.

But I HIGHLY recommend reading the first two chapters. This is a short book because I know you're busy hustling—so I wouldn't have included them if I didn't think they were valuable. But I won't be offended if you skip 'em.

Stop Spending to Start Living

Before we talk about your spending, let's talk about what you've already spent.

I want to ask you some questions. They might not seem directly related to a No-Spend Challenge, but the answers are the foundation to succeeding long term. Without them, you won't see the full benefit of doing No-Spend Challenges.

If you're going to do something difficult, then take full advantage of its lessons so you get better every time. You can only grow if you're challenging yourself, so go big or go home.

Can You Relate?

If you're anything like I was a few years ago, you may be in some state of denial about your financial situation. I avoided acknowledging my financial future by saying things like "I have plenty of time," or "everyone has student loan debt."

A year into grad school, I listened to Dave Ramsey's Financial Peace University CDs. I'd borrowed them from a friend because I couldn't afford the class. I'd just drained my bank account from a semester traveling the country and I knew I wasn't being as responsible as I could be. I was also in school and knew my anticipated debt would be over $50,000.

After finishing the series, I didn't feel motivated to pay off my debt. I just felt a panic attack coming on.

I had anxiety thinking about the rest of the student loans I'd need to take out and how much I'd have to work to be able to pay for school. A few months later, my car died—bye-bye saving for school.

I felt ashamed for willingly taking on debt so I ignored the whole concept, and kept spending. I got a car loan and took out another credit card. I knew paying off my debt was the right thing to do, but becoming debt-free felt impossible so I didn't even try to stop going into debt.

We all have skeletons in our financial closet, but more and more it seems like those skeletons are taking over our entire financial house. My debt brought with it intense feelings of guilt and shame. It restricted my choices, exhausted me, and left my self-esteem in the pits.

No wonder everyone has debt but no one wants to talk about it.

I was doing really well ignoring the whole financial thing until I met Travis. This guy wanted to pay off his student loans and wouldn't take "no" for an answer. He was never going to force me to pay off my debt, but he didn't want to live with his. He said he didn't want to settle for "getting by" and ultimately pushed me to dream about what living my life fully could look like.

For me, that was fostering.

After years of working in foster group homes, I knew I wanted to be a foster parent someday. Even after seeing firsthand how difficult, inconvenient, and heartbreaking fostering could be, I knew (and still know) it's how I want to grow our family. Because of the stress fostering can entail, I wanted options. I wanted to be able to be a stay-at-home mom, or if I wanted to work, the ability to accept a low-stress job with flexible hours.

But that plan couldn't work if we were making $1,000 in debt payments every month.

Travis got me thinking that **maybe drowning in debt doesn't have to be normal**. Connecting debt freedom to what was most important to me made the biggest difference in convincing me to face my fears about debt and pursue my dream life.

That's why I jumped on board with paying off debt and building a solid financial foundation for my family. I realized that a few years of scrimping would mean freedom for the rest of my life. Freedom not just to become a foster parent but also to forge my own path and become the person I didn't yet know I wanted to become.

Before you consider doing a No-Spend Challenge, think about what's most important to you. Not the things you want to be able to do or afford, but what you value most in life.

Dig into your core values and start to envision what a values-aligned life looks like for you. Then connect debt freedom to that life. This is sometimes referred to as "finding your 'why.'"

Figuring out why you want to pay off your debt is key to paying it off. Retirement was not enough of a reason for me. Having nice things and a nice house didn't motivate me. But the thought of being able to stay home with my future kids got me going. And when I was discouraged during the middle period of our debt payoff, imagining long-term work flexibility kept me going.

What is it for you? Is it quitting your job to start a passion project? Have more kids? Travel? Being able to give insanely generously? Figure out what you value most highly, not what other people may be telling you that you should value, and take action in the direction of your values-aligned life. **Whatever it is, be honest, be vulnerable, and be passionate about it.**

What's Keeping You From Paying Off Your Debt?

Everyone has an excuse for why they can't pay off debt. Out loud, I would say it's because I didn't make enough. And while I made less in a year than my total debt amount, that wasn't the real reason.

The real reason I didn't want to pay off my debt was FOMO: Fear of Missing Out. I didn't want to be left behind or forgotten because I wasn't spending as much money as my friends. I had no problem buying generic brands at the grocery store, but I wanted to go out with friends or take a trip without having to consult a budget that I thought would always tell me "no."

I wish managing money was as easy as saying, "spend less and earn more." Everyone would be a whiz at delayed gratification and have zero entitlement about giving up their weekends for a second job.

But the mind is a complex beast that keeps us doing things we know aren't good for us in service of irrational fears and misconceptions.

What's your excuse for not paying off your debt? You might be embarrassed to say it like I was, or you might have a really good reason. Whatever it is, you have to decide if the excuse is more important than achieving financial freedom and your values-aligned life.

These are some excuses I hear a lot when it comes to not being able to pay off debt:

"I don't make enough money."
"I couldn't pay it off even if I tried."
"I don't have time to focus on it."
"Everyone has debt."

The thing is, these excuses are backed by data or testing of any kind. You may not make enough right now to pay off your debt in two years but you can always increase your income. You may have tried and failed before but you can always gain more skills and try again.

These things are likely not keeping you in debt. They're just limiting mindsets.

To reach financial freedom you first have to figure out the false and limiting mindsets you have about money and fill your mind with the truth that destroys them. Changing your mindset will change your outlook.

There are many limiting mindsets, but the one that kept me in debt and that I see keeping a lot of other people in debt is the scarcity mentality. Scarcity mentality is seeing all resources as finite. Put another way: If one person has more, then everyone else is forced to have less.

The corporate world has trained us to think this way. Promotions and raises are scarce and must be fought for. Budgets are limited and managers hoard information. This mindset prevents us from thinking long term because we have to use all our energy to take what we can get now.

The scarcity mentality is a lie. Yes, some resources are limited, but they're probably not the ones you're focusing on. Your time, physical space, and mental energy are far more limited than your ability to earn more and spend less.

You might think you're broke, but once you make a budget, you might find you're just overspent. Think you don't have enough time to work an extra job? Maybe you need to find a better productivity strategy or find a new job with a higher salary. There is plenty of money, there are plenty of jobs, and most resources are abundant. It takes time, but once you start to think this way, you start to see opportunities you would've easily missed before. And those opportunities will help you reach your financial and life goals faster than you thought possible.

Whatever you think is keeping you from paying off your debt, I promise you someone else in a situation similar to yours has conquered the goal. You're not alone.

I'm not a person attracted to "woo-woo" kind of things. I don't believe in manifestation or anything like that. But there are multiple scientific studies to back up the idea that mindset significantly impacts the way you make short and long-term decisions.

So if you're ready to trade in your limiting mindsets for one that sets you up for financial freedom, here are three things you can do to adopt a healthier mindset.

1. Practice Gratitude

A scarcity mentality sees only limitations, so combat it by focusing on what you have and being grateful for it. A study out of UC Davis found that expressing gratitude can improve mental and physical well-being.

2. Surround Yourself With Abundance Thinkers

You will see time and time again throughout this book that you become the company you keep. When you surround yourself with people who talk about their limitations, how others limit them, and how you're limited too, all you'll see are limitations. Find people who believe a rising tide lifts all boats.

3. Look for the Win-Win

Conflicts and challenges are inevitable. Instead of assuming there has to be a win-lose solution, train your brain to look for a win-win in every challenge, even small ones. The challenge may not end with a win-win solution every time, but the more you practice this way of thinking, the more automatic it will become.

How Much Debt Are You Going to Pay Off This Year?

The Bureau of Labor Statistics divided Americans into five earning levels and studied the income-to-expense ratio for each. The bottom two groups spent more on average than what they made, while the top three groups made more money than they spent.

The lowest earners spent only about $29,000 annually.

You're probably thinking $29,000!? That's less than $2,500 per month, I can't live on that!

I get it. I'm not saying you have to live on $29,000 per year, and there are probably factors unique to your situation that would prevent it. I tell you this to encourage you to eliminate the word "can't" from your vocabulary.

I also don't say this to guilt you about spending too much. As simply as my family lived, we spent well over that every year. But if you make $40,000 per year and you're still struggling to find money to pay off debt, then I want you to see there's still hope for you.

You *can* cut your spending, You *can* go a week, month, or year without spending on more than basic needs. You are capable of reaching goals that are so much bigger than you're thinking right now.

Once you know what your values-aligned life looks like and you've confronted your limiting mindsets to believe it's possible, it's time to make the plan to get there. Now's the time to look at your debt, income, and spending and reverse-engineer your financial freedom.

Figure out the goals you need to accomplish to get there and give them deadlines. The deadline shouldn't be something stressful, but it should be a little challenging. Time limits give your brain a sense of urgency and help you stick to the plan for achieving them.

Now is an excellent time to start a journal. I wish I'd kept a journal during the first year of my debt payoff. Even as I reread this book while writing the second edition, I realized there are things I would've never thought about again without this written account.

Write about what financial freedom looks like for you, what's stopping you from earning more income, and how you feel about your purchases. Devise a plan for improving and working through your limiting mindsets, all the while keeping your current goal in mind to make sure your actions aren't arbitrary.

It's not enough to say, "Make a budget and stop spending money." If it were that easy, everyone would do it!

For the rest of this guide, I'm going to lay out the tools you need to strengthen your willpower for a no-spend challenge, stop spending on things you don't need, and use your No-Spend Challenge to improve your life. I'll give you ideas on how to use your newly found time and a little guidance for beyond the challenge.

You're going to discover what you find value in and leave behind the guilt that comes with overspending. I am so excited for you. I believe in you and know you can crush this. But you gotta believe in yourself too.

Hopefully the tips you gain here will give you more confidence to do that. Until then, focus on yourself, surround yourself with people who encourage the crap out of you, and believe in yourself as much as they do.

GO DO THE THINGS:
- Write down your "why" and find your core values
- Think about your limiting mindsets
- Make your goal and a plan to reach it
- Believe in yourself

2

Budgeting Isn't The Answer

The most talked-about issue when people are getting their finances together is sticking to a budget. There's a painful verse in the Bible where Paul writes, "I don't understand what I do. What I want to do I don't, but what I hate I do."

It sounds like Paul hated budgeting too.

Nobody makes a budget just to break it. So why do we have this problem that's been going on for thousands of years where we can't keep our commitments to ourselves? And how do we fix it?

I believe the answer lies in taking the emphasis OFF of budgeting.

You wouldn't be alone in thinking that a budget is the answer to your money problems. People love to say how their budget saved them or that living on a budget made the biggest impact on their debt payoff. And while I do believe financial freedom starts with a budget, it is not the result of it.

The reality is, your budget isn't the solution to your money problems. It's the tool that uncovers the problems.

Your budget is simply a plan and source of accountability for sticking to that plan. You can change any number on it anytime you want—you're in charge.

Budgeting is very simple. It's nice to see other people's budgets, but you're more than capable of creating a zero-based budget. More knowledge about budgeting is likely not the answer to your budgeting problem.

What you need is help to stick to your budget. That doesn't come from improving your budget. It comes from improving your lifestyle.

Your Brain is Tired

A lot of people think their addictive or impulsive personality means they can't change their overspending habits. While there's something to be said for how genetics and personality affect the purchases we make, overspending and impulsive spending aren't personality problems.

Before we dive into practical strategies for controlling your spending, let's get sciencey.

The prefrontal cortex of your brain is in charge of executive functions like logic, planning, problem-solving, and impulse control. According to a <u>study on the prefrontal cortex</u> and impulsive decision-making by the National Center for Biotechnology Information, there are two types of impulsiveness.

The first is when the brain places too much weight on immediate outcomes without considering the weight of future benefit, like in the famous test where kids have to choose one marshmallow now or two later. (Spoiler, most of them picked the immediate gratification.)

The second is the rapid response of habit without considering what the correct response *should* be. Like when I would see a Starbucks and the next thing I know, I'm in the drive-thru line.

The study further showed that people's willpower to choose the best option decreased when they were faced with stress, distraction, and even loud noises.

Got any of those in your life?

And even if for some reason you're blessed with a constant state of zen peace all the time, willpower also depletes with every decision you make, from what to wear in the morning to whether you should put cheddar or pepper jack on your sub.

Adults make around <u>35,000 decisions</u> every day, which seems crazy, but many of the decisions you make you aren't fully aware of. You decide to scratch an itch or check a phone notification out of habit more than intention, but they're still decisions. And with every decision, no matter how small, your ability to make intentional decisions depletes. This is called decision fatigue.

Decision fatigue is one of the reasons you can be successful with your No-Spend Challenge all day, then when 9 p.m. rolls around, you find yourself on your phone buying something that seems too important to wait on.

Researchers determined that willpower isn't a reservoir; it's a muscle. While you can't draw from it whenever you like (if that was true, we'd all be fit and rich) you can stretch it and strengthen it over time to go further and last longer. At the same time, you can turn decisions that take a lot of willpower into habits that become your rapid response.

No-Spend Challenges can be an exercise in strengthening your willpower to build better rapid responses. Saying no to all or most spending reduces the number of decisions you make in a day. That, in turn, gives your brain more space to make better decisions about important things. It also builds healthier spending habits that will hopefully carry over when you're done with the challenge.

Good Decisions on Autopilot

Speaking of habits, we can use habits to pick up the slack that depleted willpower and decision fatigue causes. If you're not sure what your limiting habits are, a No-Spend Challenge can help you identify them. And once you start breaking them, you can start building growth habits that put good decisions on autopilot.

For me, one of my limiting habits was takeout coffee. I'm not against coffee, I'm currently writing this in a coffee shop with an iced latte by my side. But I used to grab coffee whenever I drove past a coffee shop, whether I wanted it or not. It wasn't enjoyable, it was habitual.

Because of that, coffee was the first thing to go on my No-Spend Challenge. After a few challenges, I'd broken my coffee habit and actually began to prefer to drink my coffee at home out of one of my favorite mugs.

Now I rarely ever get coffee to go. I love a good latte, but I only get it if I'm working at a coffee shop or spending time with a friend. My coffee-buying is no longer spontaneous, it's intentional; I make sure it's something I'm looking forward to. I've figured out what works for me to make fewer decisions and develop a healthier habit.

It wasn't easy breaking the habit. To my brain the habit was neutral. All it wanted to do was make the easiest decision and expend as little energy as possible. I had to make a conscious decision every day to do things that would alert me to habit before I ended up spending the money.

What finally ended the habit were the series of No-Spend Challenges I did. Saying "no" to spending for one month at a time disrupted the habit loop that was running my brain's actions.

The habit loop is made up of three stages:
1. **Cue**, the trigger that starts the habit,
2. **Routine**, the actual act of the habit, and
3. **Reward**, the desired feeling you get by completing the habit

I like James Clear's revised version in his book *Atomic Habits* that adds craving for the reward before the routine.

My No-Spend Challenges forced me to explore my habits and get creative in how to improve them. I knew the trigger of my habit was seeing the coffee shop, but I discovered the craving was just to have something in my hand when I got to my destination. I was able to get the same reward by getting a cool travel mug.

When you're doing No-Spend Challenges, you'll have the space and time to explore the cues and cravings of your habits as well. Knowing what makes up your habits still isn't a quick fix—it's a long road to reengineer habits. But if you stay committed, you will get there.

There are four stages of habit transformation, as coined by productivity expert Carey Bentley.

Stage 1: Unconscious Incompetence

Here you're living on autopilot but you don't know you could be intentionally improving. It never gets easier seeing friends and family at this stage. But you have to remember you were there once, and this is where we all start.

Stage 2: Conscious Incompetence

This is the enlightenment stage. You can start seeing what you're doing wrong but you don't know how to improve. This is where most people linger. I was here for a long time, held back by fear—trying all kinds of things but not finding anything that worked. This is an easy stage to get stuck in.

Stage 3: Conscious Competence

You're working on improving but it's taking a lot of brainpower and effort. You can't stay here for long. This is where the No-Spend Challenge is most valuable. It's an extreme method meant to break up the monotony and make a big impact.

Stage 4: Unconscious Competence

Finally, you get to the point where you're executing healthy habits without giving them a second thought. The more you practice and strengthen that willpower muscle, the closer you get to this stage.

In the original version of this book, I said I didn't feel bad saying I hadn't reached unconscious competence with my spending yet.

I think I was a little hard on myself. We're always our worst critics. After two years of practicing a lifestyle of strict self-discipline to reach a big goal, I was acutely aware of all the ways I fell short. But with some perspective, I can see I made a ton of progress over those two years.

Still, time has shown that even though I have a lot of healthy habits, I'm not a perfect spender. After six years of working on my finances, I still make impulse purchases, I still don't like making a budget, and I will never pay for things in cash. Not all growth habits are for everyone.

You may feel stuck in incompetence for a long time, probably longer than you deserve to be. You don't start out knowing how to do everything, and even when you learn what to do, you don't do it right at first. You may even fall back into doing what you hate. So have grace for yourself and keep going. It's only when looking back will you see how far you've come.

For Best Results, Be Nice to Your Brain

Strengthening your willpower and refining your habits is hard work, so I implore you, do anything and everything you can to make the journey easier for yourself. There aren't many life hacks for doing this. I've found it mainly comes down to being nice to your brain.

Your brain is responsible for so much, but we're specifically going to focus on the part of the brain responsible for your highest cognitive functions, the prefrontal cortex.

The prefrontal cortex is in charge of guiding your memory, planning, attention, perception, and other complex cognitive and emotional behaviors. The healthier your prefrontal cortex, the better able you are to make rational and productive decisions that take you in the direction you want to go.

While you're building healthier spending habits, there are some tricks you can use to improve the function of your prefrontal cortex. Even if you feel like the universe is working against you, when your mind is clearer, you'll make better decisions and come out on top more often.

1. Manage Stress

When we started paying off our debt, I was so stressed working multiple jobs and staring at the amount of debt we were trying to pay off that I got shingles. Thank God my body stopped me from living that way because chronic stress is horrible for your decision-making brain.

Chronic stress reduces resilience, impairs memory, and shrinks your brain cells. Stress isn't just bad for the brain; it also negatively affects your heart and immune system, and speeds aging. Nobody wants that.

You can reduce stress by practicing meditation and deep breathing regularly. Studies show that just eight weeks of brief daily meditation can increase gray matter in the prefrontal cortex. That means better impulse control and a growing willpower muscle.

If you're prone to stress, avoid caffeine, alcohol, and nicotine. In addition to costing money, they're stimulants, so they increase whatever stress levels are already present in your body.

2. Bombard Yourself With Encouragement

You can't manufacture your own encouragement. You can only top this one off with a little help from your friends. And the more the better. Find friends, family, and mentors who get what you're doing and ask them to keep you accountable, but even more importantly, encouraged. And don't be embarrassed if you need more encouragement than you assume is reasonable. Everybody needs more on the front end of a big task.

Find 7-10 friends who'll text you once a month with an encouraging quote or quality they see in you. We live up to the expectations set for us, so surround yourself with people who know you can be great. And find people whom you can encourage as well. Mutually beneficial relationships are far stronger than one-sided ones.

3. Sleep More

Sleep deprivation is a type of chronic stress, so in addition to avoiding stimulant substances, try some relaxation techniques right before bed. It takes just one good night's sleep to start improving prefrontal cortex function. Studies show that 6.5-7.5 hours of sleep is optimal.

Understand that the older you get, the more care you have to take to sleep well (even in your 20s). I used to be able to have a few glasses of wine before bed, and now if I do that I wake up in the middle of the night and can't fall back asleep. Pay attention to your sleep and avoid habits that impede it.

You can also design your bedroom as a place for sleep. Make your bedroom a place of tranquility and do your work outside of it. Training your brain to think nighttime is sleep time will improve your sleep. Experts tell new moms to keep noise and light in the house during the day and quiet darkness around at night so babies will learn the difference and develop a proper sleeping schedule. If you want to sleep like one, maybe you should too.

4. Exercise

When you're stressed, you release a hormone called cortisol, which is designed to decrease your reaction time in cases of physical or mental stress. But if you're stressed because of money and life problems and you don't have any life-saving decisions to make, that cortisol just hangs around bullying your brain cells.

The best way to burn off cortisol is through physical activity.

A mere 20-30 minutes of aerobic activity can reduce cortisol levels. So when you're trying to work up the willpower to go to the gym, know that you're not just working your puff into tuff, you're getting budgeting-buff as well. (I love rhymes and I'm not sorry about it.)

Side note: Foods with a high glycemic index (GI) increase cortisol levels, which can increase stress *and* make it hard to fall asleep. If you're stressed or having trouble sleeping, try consuming foods under 55 on the GI scale.

5. Focus on One Thing at a Time

The less you have to think about and the fewer decisions you have to make, the better the decisions you make will be. That's the philosophy of the No-Spend Challenge. By focusing on one thing, you won't have to make any other discretionary decisions about money.

I love the book *The ONE Thing* by Gary Keller and Jay Papasan. I highly recommend it to anyone embarking on a major life-changing project, like paying off debt. Instead of trying to master all your goals at the same time and inching forward on each of them, the philosophy of the ONE thing is that by focusing your energy on one thing at a time you can get maximum results from it quickly and move to your next thing quicker.

So look at your goals and make sure you're focusing on just ONE at a time. if paying off debt is your ONE thing, then make it your ONE thing and cut the clutter to achieve it fast. You've only got one brain, so stop wearing it out and work it smarter, not harder.

GO DO THE THINGS:
- **Find some encouragement buddies**
- **Go to bed an hour earlier**
- **Exercise for 30 minutes**

3

Five Steps to a Successful
No-Spend Challenge

If you skipped the first two chapters, let's recap. By now you should know that good foundations, while essential, aren't enough. A goal and a budget are must-haves, and when you're confident in your core values and mindset, you know you have the right goal and budget.

But the actual execution isn't cut and dry. Life always finds a way to throw something at you that you can't plan for.

To compensate for the unexpected, we can be more intentional with our lifestyle. You can try to form growth habits and do things to keep your decision-making brain healthy. (Still easier said than done.) There are no shortcuts on the road to lifestyle transformation. You have to go through every stage of habit adoption. A growth mindset can help you stick with the journey, but it's still difficult.

Now you're here: knowing what to do but not necessarily how to do it. Thankfully, the rest of this book is dedicated to one incredibly effective strategy for doing it: The No-Spend Challenge.

There are probably a lot of ways to change your habits and stick to a budget, but No-Spend Challenges are what worked best for me—so that's what I love talking about. I've got what some people call an "addictive" personality, which isn't necessarily negative. I'm just a very "all or nothing" person.

No-Spend Challenges worked for me because I was able to be "all in." I didn't have to think about decisions. I just knew the answer was "no" and if I wanted to do something I'd have to come up with a creative alternative. Surprisingly, when I removed the impulse to say "yes" to everything, I realized I didn't want to do most of the things I was spending money on.

I don't think you need to share that personality trait with me to find challenges effective, especially when starting on your financial freedom journey. Organizing and decluttering your finances can feel overwhelming, so a clear process with defined rules (ie, as few decisions as possible) can ease some of the overthinking that takes place in the beginning.

I know that if this is what worked for me there are surely others out there who could benefit from a definitive guide on it. Before writing this book, I was confronted with the fact that what came naturally for me in doing these challenges may not come naturally for everyone. There are also a ton of things I learned as I did them that you may think were obvious.

Either way, you don't have to do everything I did. Take the ideas that work for you and leave the ones that don't, but I've included as many as possible to give you the fullest picture of what a No-Spend Challenge is, why they're beneficial, and how to do one that's as helpful as possible.

What is a No-Spend Challenge?

A No-Spend Challenge is simply a set amount of time where you don't spend any money on predetermined expenses. The key points are: You determine how long the challenge is and what you aren't spending money on.

There's also nothing keeping you from having the things you're not spending money on—you just have to get creative in trying to obtain them without spending money. I'm not suggesting you steal them! There are plenty of creative ways to get free things I'll share later in the book.

No-Spend Challenges aren't just for saving money fast. They're an opportunity for you to shake up your routines, gain space to think about your purchases, and have time to work on the things that matter most. It also reduces a significant number of decisions you make throughout the day, (even though it does create some new ones), meaning you have less decision fatigue overall while on a No-Spend Challenge.

Why Should You Do One (or More)?

There are a bunch of reasons to try a No-Spend Challenge. I'll give you my four favorites: habit loop disruption, gamification, self-determination, and confidence.

Habit Loop Disruption

Whether it be out of necessity, season, or good ol' laziness, we all allow limiting habits to build up in our lives. It takes a long season of intentionality to change course and build your life around growth habits. And even after building the habits, you still have to be cognizant to make sure you're keeping up with them, and prevent new limiting habits from creeping up.

I told you earlier that No-Spend Challenges forced me to explore my habits and get creative in how to improve them. The first step in improving them was cutting out those limiting habits. To do that I had to disrupt the habit loop. A No-Spend Challenge forces you to disrupt the loop right at the cue and craving.

Gamification

Gamification is the use of game elements in applications that are not games. Game elements can include progress tracking, badges, teammates, and challenges. A No-Spend Challenge doesn't use all of these, but it certainly gives an element of gamification to the debt payoff and financial freedom journeys.

Research has shown that different aspects of gamification do contribute to improved motivational outcomes, some more than others. Teammates were actually shown to be one of the most effective gamification elements, and they're an element I have found crucial to a successful No-Spend Challenge.

Self-Determination

Self-determination theory suggests that people are motivated to grow and change by three innate and universal psychological needs: competence, connection, and autonomy.

Competence refers to our innate desire for growth and wanting to feel like we have or are working on the skills needed for success. Connection is our need to experience a sense of belonging and attachment to other people. And autonomy is our need to feel in control of our behaviors and goals.

Self-determination has a significant impact on motivation. People with higher self-determination feel more motivated to take action because they feel that what they do will affect the outcome.

A No-Spend Challenge provides the opportunity to develop self-determination by strengthening all three of these. For a set time you're focusing on growth, you're gaining more control over your spending behaviors and momentum toward your financial goals. Hopefully, you're doing the challenge with others, or at least with others knowing about it.

Confidence

A No-Spend Challenge can be compared to fasting (some people might even call it a spending fast). So we can look at some studies on fasting and see similar psychological effects in a spending fast.

One study showed that at the end of an 18-hour fast, participants were significantly hungrier and more irritable, but had a significantly higher sense of achievement, pride, and self-control than at the start of fasting.

I don't know what's keeping you from paying off your debt or taking whatever first step you need to to reach your financial goal, but for me, it was hands-down a lack of confidence. I just didn't think I could do something that big. I had never done anything that significant before and I had no idea what I was capable of achieving.

Don't underestimate the power of confidence. Confidence in what you can do and what you're capable of. With every No-Spend Challenge, you'll gain more of that confidence. Even if you don't complete it perfectly, you'll have a starting point to compare future challenges and see your progress. Honestly, being perfect at something new is boring. You should have trouble and expect yourself to mess up.

If you're always improving, then you're always the worst you'll ever be. So give yourself grace and always be looking back at where you were so you can celebrate how far you've come.

The Five Steps to No-Spend Challenge Success

There are many ways to do a No-Spend Challenge, and while I promote taking ownership of your challenge (more on that later), I still want to lay out a framework to make things easier for you in the beginning.

This five-step framework will help you do your first challenge with the smallest learning curve possible and allow you to learn as much as possible about yourself and your spending.

Steps one and two precede the challenge, steps three and four can be prepared before the challenge but are mostly during, and step five is completed once you're done.

Each chapter will dive into the steps deeper but here's a brief overview:

1. Create the Rules
Before you start, you'll need to create the rules of your challenge. This includes how long it'll be, the expenses you will and won't spend money on, and what you'll define as success. You'll also need to plan the challenge around your life, because if you wait for the perfect time to do a No-Spend Challenge, you'll never do it.

2. Prepare
Next, you'll prepare to spend no money (zero!) on X for Y. You'll get any necessities you need in advance, find accountability, and

determine any external rewards. You'll also learn why I hate vision boards.

3. Plan
Next, you'll plan how to transition from "spending money to fulfill needs" to "fulfilling needs without spending." You already know what your biggest problem areas are going to be, so you'll make a plan in advance for solving them.

4. Do The Thing
Next, you'll look at how to fill your time and space on your no-spend challenge. You'll be shocked by how much free time you'll have when you choose not to spend money. Instead of dwelling on it, which never leads anywhere good, use your time constructively.

5. Reflect
Finally, once your challenge is over you'll reflect on it. The sooner you reflect on an experience the more accurate the reflection will be. You'll use this reflection to plan changes you want to make long-term.

I'm sure you've noticed by now that for me, money is about far more than becoming debt-free or having an arbitrary net worth goal. Money gives you the financial freedom to be able to live your dream life. That's the ultimate goal.

I want you to reach financial freedom as quickly as possible. Not by hustling day and night to become a millionaire, but by knowing what you want in the future, knowing what you want now, and figuring out what's enough to get there.

I believe No-Spend Challenges can help you do that faster than any other means out there. So I'm excited for you to dive into these five steps and experience the transformation they offer.

4

Create Your Own Rules

People get very confused when you say "No-Spend Challenge." They'll ask things like, "What do you do about your bills?," or "Are you going to eat?" When you just look at the "not spending" part it's easy to miss the most important aspect, the challenge.

While it's a given that everyone should eat and pay their bills on a No-Spend Challenge, there's no one-size-fits-all challenge. There are many ways to do them and, if done intentionally, they produce similar results. Today you might only be able to give up Target runs, but a year from now you could eat for a month without buying groceries. The point is that **this is *your* challenge** and you get to decide the parameters.

But once you decide, you have to stick to them.

There are three areas you'll have to decide parameters on challenge length, expenses, and exceptions. I'll go through options for each with pros and cons. When making your decisions, be realistic about where you are and what you're capable of at this moment.

While most people don't think they're capable of long-term accomplishments like becoming debt-free and building a $1 million net worth, the opposite is true in the short term. It even has a name: the Dunning-Kruger effect.

The Dunning-Kruger effect is a type of cognitive bias in which people believe they know more and are more capable than they actually are. Don't *overestimate* what you are currently capable of doing. Your No-Spend Challenge shouldn't be a complete overhaul of your lifestyle. It should be only slightly uncomfortable, especially if this is your first one.

I recommend giving yourself a "quick win" before you dive into a challenge you would consider intense. So look at your options, start simple, and get more complex with every challenge.

How Long Are You Going?

The first decision to make is how long your challenge is going to be. The biggest mistake you can make is putting off or shortening a challenge because of events, holidays, etc. You can always plan for exceptions, which we'll talk about soon, so don't wait for the perfect time to do a challenge.

There are always options for customizing it around obligations and making it easier during difficult seasons. These are just a few ways.

No-Spend Day(s)

These are a great way to wet your feet, but they're not as easy as they sound. You still need to plan for lunches, gas, etc. It's a bummer to fail during a No-Spend Month, but it's downright deflating to fail a No-Spend Day.

No-Spend Week

Going five or seven days without spending is where it starts to get difficult, but it can be exhilarating. You can always "accidentally" not spend on a random day, but you are guaranteed to make some hard decisions when doing this for a week.

I recommend starting on a Monday and going through Friday or Sunday. Use the Sunday before you start for grocery shopping, filling up your tank, and prepping your meals for the week. Make it as easy as possible for yourself to leave your wallet at home for the week.

No-Spend Weekend

Depending on your schedule, not spending on weekdays could be easy. It was super easy for us when we were both working three jobs and just eating snacks for dinner. The weekend is harder because it's meant to reward you for making it through another work week.

Doing a No-Spend Weekend is a great opportunity for learning how to get creative with your time and find free things to do. Your boundaries may also be tested if someone asks you to do something that costs money. These are some of the hardest things to overcome in longer challenges so don't write off the No-Spend Weekend just because it seems short.

No-Spend Month

This one's by far the most popular length and my favorite. I highly recommend trying a No-Spend Month at least once in your life. Things you can skip for a week typically can't be skipped for an entire month so you will get a really clear picture of where you're at and what you need to work on.

I think this length is probably the most difficult because you're always so close, yet so far away from the things you want. It takes a lot of self-discipline to stick to a No-Spend Month so you'll also have to deal with slip-ups and learn how to come back from them.

No-Spend Hybrid

If you want to incorporate No-Spend Challenges into your life long-term while still having some freedom to spend, the hybrid model can make challenges sustainable without losing the gamification.

The No-Spend Hybrid sets a goal number of No-Spend Days for each month. You can decide how many months in advance or decide to do it indefinitely. You're also in control of how many days you set as your goal.

I love this concept because you can make big changes without big inconveniences. If you choose to do a hybrid for a year and have 15 No-Spend Days every month, by the end you've done the equivalent of a six-month No-Spend Challenge!

While hybrids are more flexible and a great way to save money long term, they offer more money-saving and gamification benefits than they do self-discovery and self-discipline. I recommend doing at least one No-Spend Month and being very confident in what you need to work on in your spending before trying a hybrid.

No-Spend Years and Beyond

Doing a No-Spend Challenge for longer than a month is hard, but it's an extremely efficient way to change your life and bank account. And I love efficiency. Doing a challenge over multiple months means you'll likely experience every temptation your life has to offer —often multiple times—and you'll see your financial growth a lot faster.

People blog and write books about not spending for an entire year, or sometimes longer! If you're sick and tired of being in debt and ready to make a BIG change in your life, then a No-Spend Year might be right for you. Here are some great books from some amazing people who stopped spending for a year or more:

- *The No Spend Year* by Michelle McGagh

- *The Year Without a Purchase* by Scott Dannemiller
- *The Year of Less* by Cait Flanders
- *The Spender's Guide to Debt-Free Living* by Anna Newell Jones

Links to those books and every other recommendation in this book can be found at modernfrugality.com/recommendations-from-the-no-spend-challenge-guide

What's on Your No-Spend List?

Next comes deciding what you will and will not spend money on. Like I said, you should pay your bills and make sure you eat. What I'm talking about here are discretionary purchases.

The goal with a No-Spend Challenge is to shake up your routines of habitual, impulsive, and emotional purchases. So unless you're impulse buying your utilities, you don't need to focus on fixed expenses.

There are several ways you can decide to cut expenses. Here are a few.

No Spending on Particular Items

Start by looking at your transactions for the last 90 days and cutting out specific expenses that are recurring or costing you more than you'd like. You can start with one, your top three, or any number you want.

No Spending on Impulse

This one is broader than the last method but still allows for a few luxuries that are planned in advance. You're basically giving yourself a $0 personal budget. Before the month begins you'll include in your plan the times you need to work from a coffee shop or a particular sale you want to take advantage of for a certain item. Then during your challenge, you can buy only those items—and nothing else.

Spend Only on Groceries and Gas

This is the most common way I do a No-Spend Month. It's no impulse spending and no luxuries. This is an effective way to make an impact on your savings. I take it a step further by trying to clear out my pantry stockpile over the month and spend as little on groceries as possible. If you never feel like you have enough time to plan meals out of those lingering pantry items, you'll be surprised at all the extra time you have when you're not out spending money!

Pure No-Spending

This is great for short spurts, like a day or week. I wouldn't recommend this method for longer than that, but if you're really into challenges, then have at it. And let me know when you do it because I'd love to interview you about the experience. It's been four years and I'm still waiting for someone to call me on this.

Rules of Exception

The last rule is your rule of exceptions, because life happens. There are always going to be things that come up that cost money. Understanding this can eliminate the feeling of failure when your challenge doesn't go perfectly. And when you define your exceptions in advance you do the even more important work of deciding what things are NOT exceptions.

I'm not going to tell you what your exceptions may or may not be—that's personal. Some examples could be when your child needs $20 for a field trip before your challenge is over or a networking event comes up that could directly affect your job prospects in the near future. Those are very specific and time-limited.

Some things that would make bad exceptions would be general spending on your kids or work. Think about your goals and what is worth intentionally spending money on and what is not.

Chances are you will not have more than one of these come up in a month, so if you find yourself making "exceptions" several times during a challenge, reevaluate what you define as specific and time-limited. This rule is meant to allow you to take opportunities without putting off or "failing" your No-Spend Challenge, not to rationalize impulse expenses.

It would be easy for me to lay out a day-by-day plan for a 30-day challenge that you can follow without thinking about customization or exception. But for your sake, I'm not going to do that. Teaching you how to make your challenge your own gives you more ownership of it and, in turn, makes you more likely to complete it.

Psychological ownership is the feeling that something is yours. Research shows that experiencing psychological ownership enhances an individuals' self-esteem.

Ownership shapes people's judgments of themselves and their possessions and influences their behavior toward their possessions. Similar to physical possessions, psychological ownership influences how we treat ideas, projects, responsibilities, etc. The more you feel like you own the idea, the more you're motivated to carry it out.

Simply put, customizing your No-Spend Challenge is a small trick for increasing your commitment to it. So don't look for someone else to tell you how to spend your days—you probably won't do it anyway. Forge your own path and feel a higher sense of accomplishment when you're able to succeed on it.

GO DO THE THINGS:
- **Decide the length of your next challenge**
- **Write down what you will and will not spend on during it**

5

Prepare to be Amazed

"The essential thing 'in heaven and earth' is that there
should be **a long obedience in the same direction**;
there thereby results, and has always resulted in the long
run, something which has **made life worth living**."
—Friedrich Nietzsche

The things that make life worth living demand long obedience
in the same direction. It's not always an exciting road, but the
things that bring the most value are at the end of it.

Financial freedom takes a long time. There are many routes to
financial freedom but one thing is certain: you have to choose
your route and stick to it. Flip-flopping every time you see someone on Instagram or TikTok propose a new idea will only leave
you worse for wear.

I've found that sticking with anything comes down to how well you prepare for it. When your willpower is depleted and you have the opportunity to solve your problem by spending money, you have to make following your challenge as easy as possible.

There are three things you need to prepare in advance: Your budget, accountability, and motivation.

The Good, The Bad & The Budget

Americans paid $12.4 billion in overdraft fees in 2020, and 80% of those fees are paid by the same group of people.

Small tangent: I believe that with the technology we currently have, overdraft fees are now an unethical money grab for banks. They disproportionately target low-income bank users and contribute to cyclical poverty. Even if you're not one of the 80% of the people paying frequent overdraft fees, you should move your money to a bank or credit union that doesn't charge them. More are popping up all the time. I'll include my updated favorites on the recommendations page for this book, which you'll find at modernfrugality.com/recommendations-from-the-no-spend-challenge-guide.

Getting all your bills and expenses down on paper, in an app, or on a spreadsheet makes you aware of your purchases so you can avoid paying for carelessness. It can also make you self-aware. You may assume your income forces you to live paycheck-to-paycheck but your budget can challenge that if it shows you "should" have money to save.

So it's necessary to have a budget before, during, and after your challenge. I recommend a zero-based budget. You can find plenty of tutorials on how to make one online, but the gist of it is that you spend every dollar of your income starting with bills, then funding financial goals, and then discretionary spending. The only thing that should change about your budget during a No-Spend Challenge is taking out some or all of the discretionary spending and transferring that amount to funding financial goals.

You'll also need to adjust your budget before you start to get necessities. Look around your house to see if anything is going to run out while you're on your challenge like toiletries, cosmetics, pantry, and kitchen items. If anything's running low, grab it before the month begins so you don't tempt yourself with extra shopping trips.

People love looking at other people's budgets and comparing their spending to others, so while I'm sure you'd love to see an example of my budget or at least a sample budget, I'm not going to give it to you. Budgets are extremely subjective based on countless factors from income and where you live to how many kids you have or whether you're caring for a family member.

It will not help you to see another picture of another budget.

What will help you is to inspect your own budget as thoughtfully as possible. See what you can take out easily, see what you can negotiate or shop around for better rates, and ask difficult questions about expenses you feel you "need" or are "fixed." Your core values aren't fixed—they change and you discover new ones, so you will always be refining your budget.

The key takeaway here is no matter how "ugly" your budget is, make one every month.

While you're on your No-Spend Challenge, spend your money as soon as it comes in. Use this time as an opportunity to catch up or get ahead. Pay your bills early, make an extra debt payment, transfer money to a different account, whatever.

You can still pay off your debt *and* suck at budgeting, but you can't forget the budget altogether. It's an essential part of the equation and makes the process faster and easier, even if it doesn't seem that way all the time.

If life gets crazy and you muck it up, fix it and move on. Don't wait until the next month to try again or give up. Just keep going. And use No-Spend Challenges as a way to refine your budget more and more every year.

Fast Alone, Further Together

You may be familiar with the quote from Jim Rohn that goes, "You're the average of the five people you spend the most time with."

It's a call to audit the people around you and make sure you're spending time with people who are living in alignment with what you want for your own life. The idea encourages you to spend time with people further ahead on their journey to raise your "average."

Time and time again I've seen that statement to be true. The more I hang out with my gym friends the more often I work out. The more successful business owners I follow on Instagram the more motivated I am to grow my business. I even find myself adopting a slight southern accent after several days with my family in Alabama and Georgia.

A study on smoking took this concept further to see not just how significant your immediate network is on your behaviors, but how much of an influence *your network's network* has. It seems silly to consider your friend's friends having any influence on how you live your life, but the results say to some extent, they do.

Twelve thousand people assessed repeatedly from 1971 to 2003 showed that discernible clusters of smokers and nonsmokers extended to three degrees of separation.

Even with a decrease in smoking in the overall population, the size of the clusters of smokers remained the same across time, suggesting that those who were quitting were doing it in groups, whether they realized it or not.

The study found that if a participant's friend smoked, they were 61% more likely to be a smoker. If a friend of their friend smoked, they were 29% more likely to smoke. And if a friend of a friend smoked they were still 11% more likely to smoke.

Why this phenomenon? Your greater network, even the people you don't know directly, impact your perception of what's acceptable.

We all want to be accepted and part of a group and we'll do as much (or as little) as necessary to be accepted by the groups available to us. If you want to smoke but none of your friends smoke, you're more likely to quit. But if your non-smoking friend has friends who smoke, you know you'll still be accepted by that person and be less motivated to quit.

How does this relate to a No-Spend Challenge? You go further if you intentionally surround yourself with people managing their money well and who have friends who are successful with money.

This doesn't mean going out and only having rich friends. It means you have to be intentional with who you spend your time with and who you follow on social media. Further, be conscious of the kind of people they spend time with and what they share on social media. Because if you see it it will affect you, whether you're on or off a No-Spend Challenge.

Find people who will not just support your efforts to improve your money management and pursue financial freedom, but who are doing it themselves.

That's why you shouldn't be embarrassed to tell everyone you're doing a No-Spend Challenge.

Some people will think you're weird for doing it, but if you tell others, you give them permission to be weird too. When you're doing the challenge to improve your spending habits (not because you're broke), you'll inspire others who may want to do better with their money but are afraid to start.

Telling people also helps your friends avoid awkward situations. People with the best intentions for you will probably ask you to spend money with them. Hopefully, you'll say no, but making your challenge known will keep these temptations and awkward situations to a minimum.

Most importantly, telling people will allow you to find an accountability partner(s). They don't necessarily need to do the challenge with you, but they can be your encouragement buddies. Local partners are always best, but the internet can provide great relationships too.

I've found Instagram to be a great place to declare your challenge and find encouragement. Hashtags like #debtfreecommunity, #nospend, and #nospendmonth will show you what other people are doing and how they're doing it. Instagram has proven to be an awesome community of people tracking their debt freedom progress and pitfalls. Some accounts I highly recommend following:

- @inspiredbudget
- @lydiasenn
- @gobudgetgirl
- @clobaremoneycoach
- @debtfreegonnabe
- @frugalfriendspodcast (#shamelessselfpromotion)

Motivation, Elevated

No-Spend Challenges are a catalyst for motivation. That's what we're all looking for, right? Good habits on autopilot and motivation to do the right thing for everything else?

What people don't realize is that there are two types of motivation, external and internal, and you need both in different ratios.

When it comes to motivation we often focus on the external: any motivating factor that comes from outside of you. External rewards include a nice dinner, an accountability partner cheering you on, or the money you earn from working. These are effective early on in your journey, but the more time passes, the less effective they become.

What then picks up the slack are internal motivators, which are typically derived from your core values.

I own my own business so nobody is going to care if one day I decide I don't want to work. Money is a nice external motivator, but we live on one income so we don't technically need it. I work because I absolutely LOVE what I do. It fulfills or helps me fulfill all my core values.

I've quit many things over the years that were profitable because I just didn't like doing them. But I love Monday mornings and doing what I do, even if I'm not making as much money as I used to.

A No-Spend Challenge is an external motivation technique for discovering internal motivators. You can use the challenge to gamify your experience and save up a sweet pile of cash to put toward your financial goal. And you can probably expect your friends and family to congratulate you after—even more external motivation.

Meanwhile, the whole time you're on the challenge you're going to be discovering what you value most and what you don't care as much about. You'll be testing your "why" to see if it's truly your purpose or the one that's been projected onto you. You'll be developing internal motivators that you'll carry long after your challenge is over.

That is the reason I love No-Spend Challenges so much. You can't stick to a budget you don't love, and you don't know the budget you're capable of living on without testing yourself. Life tests us when we least expect it, and in the chaos, it can take years to learn the lessons we were meant to take from it.

While internal motivation is more important long-term, both are important during a No-Spend Challenge. So before you start, prepare your strategies for external and internal motivation. Look for free ways to reward yourself and plan a small reward for after the challenge that may or may not cost money.

For internal motivation, write your "why" on an index card or draw/collage it on a poster board. Whatever you need to remind yourself that this is about more than just a few extra dollars in your bank account. Keep it with you, post it on your bathroom mirror, in your car, or all of the above.

Whatever you do, avoid making a "dream board," or what I like to call a "stuff I want to spend money on but can't right now so I will torture myself with that reminder" board. When creating a visual representation of your "why" and core values, only include things money can't buy. Those are the real internal motivators. Pictures of sandy beaches and new cars will only give you FOMO and actually distract you from your goals.

GO DO THE THINGS:
- **Make your budget**
- **Find out what you need for the month and purchase it**
- **Declare your #nospendchallenge on Instagram and Facebook**
- **Plan your motivators**

6

Plan... Then Throw The Plan Away

I love this scene in the TV show *The Flash* when Flash recruits Leonard Snart to help him steal a power source from ARGUS. In their preparation for the heist, Snart has this brilliant sentiment:

> "Make the plan. Execute the plan. Expect the plan to go off the rails. Throw away the plan."

The fact is, you can make a very good budget, have great accountability and motivators, and eventually, you're going to mess up or life is going to do it for you. And that's ok. If that doesn't happen then you're probably not challenging yourself enough. So what do you do when the plan goes off the rails?

Keep going.

Falling off the wagon, no matter how far, is not an excuse to give up and try again next month. Commit to getting back on that wagon, going further, and failing better next time.

In a study published by the *European Journal of Social Psychology*, a researcher studied 96 people trying to build a new habit over 12 weeks. It took those people an average of 66 days for their new small task to feel automatic. The longest took 254 days!

The study also showed that a few missed days didn't affect how long it took to build the habit. What made the difference was how quickly they recommitted. The more your mind and actions have to change, the longer it will take a new habit to take root. You can succeed, but you will fail first.

Let your mess-ups teach you what to do better next time. If you had a bender at Target on your last challenge, you know not to go to Target during your next. If the coffee shop on your way to work killed your streak, put coffee in your hand before you leave the house. If lunch is your downfall, do more meal prep next time. That way if (and when) you fail again, it's less and less of a big deal.

If the car breaks down or your kid gets sick, you can press pause, make the necessary purchases, then get back on track. Responding to an emergency doesn't mean you have to give up.

Gone are the days of self-loathing and shame for not executing your plan perfectly. You're learning to be better, and no change happens overnight. It doesn't even happen in 21 days.

To limit (unwarranted) feelings of deflation when the plan goes awry, I've got another three strategies for you: Anticipate surprises, say "the magic word," and find $0 solutions to problems.

Surprise!

It may seem counterintuitive, but a lot of surprises can be anticipated. Sit down and look at your calendar from the last 30 days. What unexpected things came up every day? Did you get asked to an impromptu happy hour? Was there a surprise weekend sale? Did your in-laws show up on your doorstep and volunteer you to take them to dinner?

Identifying "recurring surprises" is another reason to develop a daily journaling habit. Simply taking an account of your day can show you how predictable some of your unexpected expenses are.

If you haven't started daily journaling, look at your last 30 days of transactions and try to journal a sentence for every day based on what you can remember about those expenses. This will help you plan your response, or an alternative solution, for every one that could come up again on your No-Spend Challenge.

It's hard to be creative on the spot, but if you plan ahead, you don't have to summon that creativity, which better ensures that you stick with the challenge. And if you're having trouble introducing your creative response or alternative, you can always fall back on the magic word.

The Magic Word

If nothing else, there's one thing you'll get very good at saying on a No-Spend Challenge: "No."

But that's not the magic word by a long shot.

If saying "no" was easy, everyone would do it (and furthermore, we'd all be fit.) That's why I like the real magic word: "But."

It's a magical word that takes "no" from a depriving evil word and turns it into a benign annoying word.

Here are some examples:

> "I can't do that, **but** what about this?"
> "I'm not spending money right now, **but** wanna come over to my place?"
> "I REALLY want it, **but** I'll wait until the challenge is over to get it."
> "I usually do this, **but** I could save some money if I tried that."

We tend to live in a world of declaring absolutes. Like, "Starting today I'll 'always' make a budget" or "I'm 'never' going to buy that again." But the truth is, it's way easier to live in the "not now, but later" mindset.

The rest of this chapter is filled with all the "buts" I could come up with.

These "buts" will hopefully help you retrain your brain and body to replace unhealthy spending habits. Don't live in the world of "I don't have time to cook so I have to spend money eating out" or "my kids do a lot of activities and it adds up."

Learn the alternatives, come up with some of your own, and start spending better.

$0 Solutions to $1,000 Problems

What is it that drives us to revert to eating out when we're tired or bored? Some people say it's fun to get dressed up and go to a restaurant, or it's easier to have someone serve your food and remove the dishes.

If you think about it, eating at home is just as "fun" as eating out, and expends the same amount of energy. When you go out, you drive there, sit down, pick your entrée, second-guess the price, order it anyway, eat, box up leftovers, grimace at the bill, and then drive home.

When you eat at home, you have to chop some vegetables and wash some dishes, but you spend less, have more leftovers, can customize your dish, can eat it in your pajamas while watching a movie, *and* you learn a skill that gets better every time you practice.

Our fear of cooking and disdain for dishes costs us almost $3,000 every year. That comes down to about $250 per month or $57 per week. Does that sound like a lot, or is that conservative for you?

Avocado toast isn't the problem. The notion that we need to spend money to have quality experiences is the problem. What could you do with an extra $3,000? How much faster would you pay off your credit cards, car, or student loans? Is the thought of that amount enough to make you cut back or quit spending on eating out altogether?

The three highest discretionary expenses for the American family are food, discretionary products and services, and entertainment. In 2019 the average family spent over $16,000 on these categories combined. While you can't (and shouldn't) cut 100% of any of these categories, cutting them by just 25% can save you an extra $4,000 after a year.

If you're earning the median average income in the U.S. of $67,000 that's a 6% increase in savings! And that $4,000 becomes even more if you're putting it toward paying off debt or investing.

Skipping the bar and Chipotle doesn't mean you can't enjoy life or never step inside a restaurant again. I enjoy eating out and for some reason, I love paying to torture myself with CrossFit and half marathons. But I've also found some creative zero-dollar solutions for expensive problems that will help you enjoy sticking to your No-Spend Challenge.

$0 Food Solutions

The goal isn't necessarily to spend $0 on food, though you can do a pantry challenge, the real goal is to avoid impulse spending at the grocery store, takeout and restaurant/ bar purchases. Here are my best tips to avoid spending money on unnecessary food and beverages.

Plan Your Meals

The number one reason for eating out is a failure to plan. That's why meal planning is so important. I have a dry-erase board on my fridge with meals listed for the week so I know what I'm going to make and when I'm going to make it. I look at the prep time each meal is going to take and plan the longer ones for the weekend and quick meals on weeknights.

I search for ingredients I already have on Pinterest to find new ways to use them. I use a meal planning service to save time but it used to take me about an hour on Sunday to plan every meal for the week. I easily got that hour back throughout the week by knowing what to make and having everything I need to make it.

Grocery Shop Online

In 2017 very few people were grocery shopping online. It was difficult to find and pricey. Today the system has totally transformed. Almost every grocery store has some kind of online component, delivery isn't required, and some are fee-free.

I've been grocery shopping exclusively online since 2019 and find it's a great way to eliminate impulse purchases. I use Walmart as it's very close to my house and offers free pick up but if you can shop at a discount grocery store online, like Aldi, a small fee might be worth it.

Use Up Your Pantry

Could you go a whole month just shopping from your pantry? We're pretty minimalist, and I know we could go for at least a few weeks. The pantry challenge is a complementary challenge to the No-Spend Month.

Emptying your pantry can tell you a lot about your spending habits. Is your pantry full of good intentions quickly forgotten, new things you took a chance on but have been avoiding, or stuff your mother-in-law sent you home with on your last visit? Whatever it is, this is a great time to use up the back row of the pantry.

Prep Freezer Meals

This is something I love even when I'm not doing a No-Spend Challenge. Making 4-6 different freezer meals using similar ingredients can keep healthy meals on your menu without buying fresh produce every week.

I'm very picky about freezer meals. My favorite freezer meals are slow cooker soups, stews, and chilis. Simply put all the chopped and ready ingredients into a gallon Ziploc freezer bag and throw it into the freezer. When you're ready, take the bag off and put the frozen block directly into the slow cooker or pressure cooker. If you freeze it upright it should fit perfectly; otherwise, you can throw it into the microwave until it melts down to fit. I use a pressure cooker so it's fine to use pre-frozen raw meat but avoid frozen raw meat if you're using a slow cooker.

I also use premade freezer meals from the grocery store. Wednesday is pizza night in our house because Travis and I both work late. Popping a pizza in the oven is easy and something we look forward to every week. Always keep your freezer full of ready-made meals. It makes for an easy dinner and a packed freezer lowers the electric bill for your fridge!

Pack Your Lunch at Dinnertime

After dinner is cooked or while it's cooking, go ahead and make lunches for the next day. If you're making a sandwich or salad, make enough for the rest of the week. Separate the soggy elements so they don't sit on your sandwich for days.

And learn to embrace the leftovers. When you're putting everything away instead of putting it in a single container, portion it out to individual-serving Tupperware. I recommend getting glass containers so you can store them, microwave them, and eat them out of the same bowl. #lessdishes

Recreate Your Faves

Do you know what's awesome? Coffee. You know what's more awesome? A makeshift latte in a fun mug in the "coffee shop" corner of your house! Sometimes I have to psychologically trick myself into thinking I'm somewhere I'm not. Seriously though, if you prefer lattes but can't throw down the daily $5 for hot foamy milk, don't fret, you can do it at home.

My old roommate taught me this trick. Heat your milk in a microwave-safe mug, then froth it with a $10 frother. Pour it over some strongly brewed coffee and voila! Latte! You can use the same concept for food. There are plenty of restaurant copycat recipes online.

Have Friends Over

During one of our No-Spend Challenges we ran into friends we hadn't seen in a long time and wanted to hang out. We didn't want to wait until the next month so we were open with them about our spending freeze and invited them over. Not only were they excited about it—they offered to make dinner and bring it over.

A week later we had another couple agree to have us at their house to hang out and watch TV. An hour before we were supposed to go over, I got a text saying they were tired, so they were just going to go out to eat (at their favorite pricey sit-down restaurant) and lay low after... but we were welcome to join.

Your real friends want to hang out with you, not just on their terms. They want to build you up and encourage you in your goals even if their own goals are different. The No-Spend Challenge transforms more than your spending. It also transforms your relationships.

So if you want to have experiences with your friends, don't be afraid to invite them over for coffee or a meal. Your house isn't as small, messy, or dingy as you think it is—and even if it is, your friends won't mind. And eventually, you'll be inviting the friends who stick with you to your dream house with comfy couches, a roomy kitchen, and a pool in the backyard.

Use Better Ingredients & Methods

I hesitate to reveal this, but I have a regular, old automatic coffee maker. I hope this doesn't change how you feel about me. I can feel my barista's judgment just thinking about it.

But if you don't like the taste of automatically brewed coffee, you don't have to suffer through it to save money. For the same price as a pot brewer, you can get several different types of "advanced" brewers.

Huffington Post tested nine methods of brewing coffee and found that Chemex produced the best-tasting cup. Spending a little more on beans and a brewer can save you money long term by avoiding the coffee-shop price markup.

You can also switch to fresh herbs or better quality ingredients from the grocery store. Again, It might increase your grocery bill at first but if it keeps you from eating out then you've saved overall.

Go on Picnics

When you want to get out of the house for a great sunset or cooler weather (something we Floridians always look forward to), you should be able to! But you don't need to pay for a seat at a restaurant to do it.

Pack all the random snack foods you would've eaten for dinner anyway (just me?) and have a relaxing picnic. Enjoy it at a park, beach, or random parking garage rooftop—just use the free street parking before heading up. Picnics are popular in France and Italy so, theming your picnic is totally acceptable.

One day you'll be able to afford that European vacation, but until then, there's no harm in pretending.

Take Surveys For Gift Cards

Taking surveys is my least favorite way to make money. But survey companies that give out gift cards instead of cash tend to make accumulating "points" a little easier.

Swagbucks is probably my favorite. Every 500 Swagbucks (SB) are approximately $5, and you can redeem them for gift cards to restaurants or a virtual MasterCard gift card. It's good anywhere, so you don't technically need to spend it at a restaurant—but you totally could.

There are a lot of survey companies out there. I don't recommend signing up for all of them; just pick the one you like and stick with it to maximize your rewards.

Go Mystery Shopping

I love mystery shopping. We don't do them on shorter challenges like a No-Spend Month but for longer challenges, they're a great treat night. You pay upfront for your meal, but once you complete your evaluation you get reimbursed, and sometimes paid extra.

Like survey sites, it's not a lucrative side hustle, but you get paid a little and reimbursed up to a certain amount, which often makes your dinner or outing free!

I do a lot of restaurant shops to scratch the itch of going out. You might think you won't be able to enjoy your meal if you're watching out for everything, but that's not the case. Companies want you to look like a regular patron so most of the details for your report are gathered at the beginning and end of the meal.

The report and narrative usually take about an hour to complete and it's best to do it right when you get home. Sometimes you'll even get a bonus for turning it in early.

Drink Less

The Mayo Clinic suggests no more than 400 milligrams (mg) of caffeine—or four 8-ounce cups of coffee—per day. In perspective, a grande coffee at Starbucks has 330 mg of caffeine, and a venti has 415 mg! Count that extra shot of espresso with 64 mg or the soda you had with 29 mg of caffeine and you're dangerously close to some bad health side effects.

And I love a good whiskey or gin and tonic but even drinking at home adds up.

I know we're all guilty of overindulging, but if you're doing it consistently, it's time to start cutting back. For your wallet *and* your health. Consider breaking up your coffee intake to 200 mg in the morning and 200 mg after lunch, then avoiding other drinks with caffeine. And limit yourself to one alcoholic drink a day or only with friends.

$0 Shopping Solutions

Step away from the computer and put down your credit card.

Shopping online is the easiest thing since sliced bread. The internet is faster than ever, marketing funnels have a solution for every hesitation you're feeling, and Amazon, oh Amazon, it knows everything I've ever wanted and the things I'm going to want.

The amount of innovation that's come out of companies like Amazon and Walmart to get us to buy more with less thought is mind-blowing. There's a reason Jeff Bezos, CEO of Amazon, is the richest man in the world.

Convenience comes with a price.

For the person in debt, the ease of shopping online can be more than a budget-buster. The satisfaction of packages on your doorstep can unravel everything you've worked for. While I'm a huge fan of online shopping, I think we need to make it harder for ourselves to do it.

We need to bring to the online shopping world the element of thought and consideration that comes with a literal full cart in a store. And thankfully, I'm not the only one who feels this way.

In addition to easy tips to reduce your exposure, you can take it a step further with plugins and services that give you an added layer of protection against the "shiny new" of the online shopping experience.

Unsubscribe From Emails

Gmail has this great feature that puts the "unsubscribe" button at the top of the email. You don't even have to look at all the cute shoes you're missing out on as you unsubscribe!

There are some subscriptions I want to keep, but those can also pose the biggest threat to my bank statement. For those, I use a free service called Unroll.Me to "roll-up" all the emails I want to stay subscribed to, but don't want to be tempted by in my inbox. It also allows me to choose to unsubscribe, roll up into a daily email, or keep in my inbox every new subscription and keeps my inbox a productive place.

Remove Apps From Your Phone

Mobile internet use has now surpassed desktop usage, so retailers are offering incentives like special discounts and early access to sales to get *their* app onto *your* phone. The easiest way to put a little distance between you and the cart is to delete the app.

I suggest going a step further and deleting, or at least hiding your social media apps. A popular tactic in marketing is "word-of-mouth marketing" or "influencer marketing." Companies use referral programs to get your friends to show off their products in hopes that you'll buy them.

Even with no incentive, my friends are always posting new gadgets and outfits on Instagram and Facebook that make me immediately want to hand over my money. So even if you don't see a direct correlation between online shopping and social media, it's there.

And I promise spending less time on social media will magically help you spend less.

Remove Your Credit Cards From Your Browser's Autofill

Feature

I love the autofill feature in my web browser. It makes every-thing faster, except when sometimes it thinks my first name is "Female." But otherwise, it's great for filling out redun-dant forms.

Even when I leave my cards at home on a No-Spend Challenge, my computer is happy to help me out by storing my card info. The solution to this is deleting them from autofill. It'll be incon-venient for some things, but worth it in the end.

On the bright side, loan servicers save bank information inter-nally so you won't need your card to make more debt payments. The same for your utility bills or other monthly expenses that are set to an automatic payment schedule.

Block Websites

There's no shame in my website-blocking game. I don't struggle with this as much anymore, but if I feel like there's a site that poses a threat to my willpower then I'll block it.

It's almost sad that there's a market for extensions and apps like this but hey, like I said, marketers are good at their jobs. These sites and their advertisements are designed, even customized, to appeal to your weak spots. So I highly recommend working smarter, not harder, with these productivity tools.

Some of my recommendations are StayFocused, LeechBlock, and Freedom but new ones come out all the time.

$0 Entertainment Solutions

After doing a few of these, I've noticed my biggest downfall during a No-Spend Challenge is getting bored at home.

I got nervous telling friends I'm not spending money, even though it was no secret we were trying to pay off debt. Here are some of my favorite free ways to get out of the house with friends or by myself.

The Library

The library is a treasure trove of fun. It's grown from novels and encyclopedias to include eBooks, DIY books, CDs, movies, museum tickets, and more. I've discovered amazing recipes and learned macramé, and my husband, who doesn't love reading, has even gotten in on it recently.

You don't even have to search high and low for what you want. Most public libraries have their databases online for you to search from the comfort of your home and request a hold on any item. They'll deliver it to the library of your choice (some even to your home) and alert you when it's ready. Easy peasy!

Social Running Group

Most running stores do group runs, and there's usually one every night of the week. Before we became parents we used to do one called Running For Brews. They do a 5K(ish) run that starts and ends at a bar. Trust me when I say all levels of runners/walkers/joggers participate. And since the pack disperses pretty quickly, it's easy to cut your run short and not be noticed (not like I ever do that...).

It's a great activity to do with friends and to make new friends, as runners are a very welcoming bunch. After the run, everyone meets back at the bar and hangs out. There's an even balance of people drinking and not drinking afterward, so it's not awkward to skip the beer purchase.

Yelp Events

Did you know Yelp hosts events? Most cities have a community ambassador who hosts Yelp events. Most are for Yelp "Elites" but occasionally they host events open to everyone. They are awesome, free, and make a great night out.

They typically include free food from local restaurants, free (alcoholic) drinks, and lots of free Yelp swag. One even gave us an hour of unlimited game play at an arcade, so fun!

You have to be diligent in checking for these official Yelp events because they always fill up. When you find one, RSVP on the event page, then wait for a confirmation email. There are no +1s, so everyone has to RSVP and get confirmation individually to attend together.

You can also apply to be Yelp Elite and have access to the exclusive Elite events. It's free to join, but you have to have a pretty impressive Yelp profile to be selected.

Bike Ride

Self-explanatory. We love a good bike ride. We live right off a trail and it's another great exercise activity to do with your significant other, friends, or just by yourself. Just like running clubs, cities have numerous biking clubs most days of the week that range in speed/experience.

Home Improvement Class

Home Depot offers free weekly workshops on everything from installing light fixtures and tile to water conservation hacks to making a DIY dog feeder. Even if you don't own a home, these are great tricks to have up your sleeve for when that time comes.

Nowadays the classes are live-streamed online but you may be able to find a class in your area at a local home improvement store. Even though I have my handy husband, it's empowering to know that if something breaks I can fix it, or if he's at work I can install it. There's something to be said for the confidence (and frustration) completing a home improvement project can bring.

Events in the Park

We live in a city that loves to be outside, and that means tons of orchestra nights, movies on a big screen, fireworks, and parades, to name a few. We love bringing a blanket, some chairs, and a picnic for the evening. Find your city's event calendar or downtown blog to find out what's available.

Volunteer

Volunteering is an amazing way to become bolder (hi, introverts) and do something for free that helps others and makes you feel good. We volunteer at our church and a foster group home in our area.

I love Habitat For Humanity (make use out of those home improvement classes!) and Big Brothers, Big Sisters. There are options for all time commitments. And it's not limited to humanitarian groups. You can volunteer at events like music and food festivals for a couple of hours then enjoy the rest of the event for free!

Game Night

Games are the gifts that keep on giving. They're reusable (as long as you can keep track of the pieces) and always a new experience.

Everyone has a copy of Monopoly but oh, my friend, games have evolved since we were kids.

Some <u>games we love</u> that are good for groups big and small are Saboteur, Settlers of Catan, and Munchkin. You'll be arguing about game-playing strategies for weeks.

Exercise

The accessibility of online workouts makes it easy to do at home by yourself or with friends. YouTube has hundreds of different types of workouts, there are blogs dedicated to home fitness, and the library lends out workout DVDs. You can also ask to borrow a friend's workout DVDs or if they'd do them with you.

Pick up an Old Hobby

Remember that hobby or Pinterest craft you bought all the stuff for, but never finished? I'm sure your friends have one too. This is a great time to gather all that yarn, lace, hot glue, and fabric and make something beautiful.

And if you're not the crafty type, adult coloring books are actually really fun. If you don't have a spare coloring book hanging around, but do have a computer printer, you can easily find free coloring sheets online to print and try.

Start a Group

About seven months into being married and paying off our debt, Travis and I were feeling pretty isolated. It's hard to reestablish normal life as a newlywed and create a new money-conscious life when your friends are obsessed with going out. So we decided we needed to embrace our new selves and find others who'd do the same.

We started a bible study with some friends at church and met at a different house every week. Even though we were working three jobs each, we knew that sharing the journey with people we love was just as important as being financially responsible.

Maybe a bible study isn't your thing; maybe it's a book club or fan meetup. Groups that meet weekly are key for us introverts to come out of our shells and get to know people. Whatever it is, I highly recommend identifying and killing your "busy" mentality to make room for more of what matters.

Murder Mystery Party

I once ended up at a murder mystery party by accident. Everyone was dressed in period costumes and I was running around in jeans trying to solve these clues with people I'd never met. It started awkwardly but it turned out to be genuinely fun.

I'm not saying you have to dress up and talk in accents, but pretending to be someone you're not is a great ice breaker and a unique way to spend an evening. Who knows, maybe murder mystery parties can become your thing on No-Spend Challenges?

GO DO THE THINGS:

- Make your list of "anticipated" surprises
- Prep your meals and ingredients for the week
- Take your credit card information out of autofill
- Find or plan a free activity with friends

Do The Thing

When I started doing No-Spend Challenges, I figured if I was going to save all this money by not spending, I wanted to "go big or go home" with it. I made it my goal to earn and save as much as possible too.

I found that having this goal helped me in two ways. The first was having more money to put toward debt when the challenge was over. The second was filling my spare time. Eventually, I added decluttering to my list of time-filling activities. Because I spent the extra time the challenge gave me with being productive instead I was never sitting around dwelling on how bored I was.

We've been consumer debt-free for over four years and I've continued with some of these practices and side hustles because I like them. So if you're going to do a No-Spend Challenge, then do the dang thing. Don't just fill your time with watching Netflix, use the forced pause to incorporate more growth-oriented habits into your life.

Here are my best tips for productively filling your time throughout a No-Spend Challenge.

Side Hustling

When we started paying off debt, I thought I had no marketable skills to "hustle" with. But I knew the only way we were going to pay the debt off fast was to make more money.

It doesn't matter how much you save. At some point, you realize it's all nickels and dimes if you're not bringing more dollars into the house.

And I'm saddened whenever I talk to people who don't want to or think they can't make extra money because of schedules, skills, or space. Not every job is right for every person, but there will be ways to make extra money that are right for you.

You just gotta keep looking and be patient.

And there's no better time to start a new side hustle adventure than when you're trying to avoid spending money. Take advantage of your "forced" free time and find a new way to make money that works for you.

Luckily, I've done a ton of side hustles with my seemingly "no marketable skills" and most have no startup costs. What they do require is start-up effort. The most lucrative ones are going to require you to research, try, and learn, for several months before you can start making money with them. This is the perfect time to do that!

Here are some ideas and websites for making a side income that's worth your time and will move the needle on your debt. Some require more start-up education than others. Online courses are a great way to bypass the learning curve but avoid buying one while you're on your challenge. I assure you even courses that "close their doors" will open them again at a later date, and if they don't there's always another that will. Do as much free research as possible before you invest in a course.

Ways to Make Extra Money by Offering Freelance Services

- Offer freelance writing services
- Become a virtual assistant
- Become a virtual bookkeeper
- Do audio editing for podcasts
- Do video editing for YouTubers and social media influencers

Ways to Make Extra Money Renting & Reselling

- Resell large and commercial items on eBay
- Flip furniture and selling through Facebook Marketplace
- Resell designer and premium clothing and accessories on Poshmark
- Offer a room/ your house on Airbnb or Homestay

Ways to Make Extra Money Semi-Passively

- Create designs and sell them on shirts or prints
- Create a course and sell it to an audience (you can build it through a podcast or Youtube channel)
- Write a fiction or nonfiction book series and publish it on Amazon
- Create a niche website for affiliate marketing
- Create a free app and sell advertising space within

When you're thinking about making extra money for your financial goals, consider that short-term saving and paying-off goals require earning methods that have a quick return while long-term goals like retiring early require more sustainable strategies.

There are a lot of websites and apps like driving for Uber or delivering food with DoorDash that give you a very quick return on your efforts and they're the best when you're starting to pay off debt. But they won't make you a lot. Offering freelance services in an area you're already proficient in is a better return on your time investment. It takes a little longer to start seeing the money, but it's much quicker than starting a business from scratch.

Passive income, on the other hand, is much better than freelancing in terms of sustainability. So if you want to leave your job one day and that's more important to you than paying off debt, then you may want to set wheels in motion for creating something you can sell semi-passively. You may not see any profit while you're paying off debt but by the time you finish, you'll be on your way to replacing your full-time income.

Spend Time Saving Money

My favorite way to save money is to spend time making it. My second favorite way is to focus on lowering a few big costs. Discretionary expenses collectively can be a big one and that's why I love No-Spend Challenges, but what about "fixed" expenses and bills?

There are plenty of ways you lower those too. And focusing on a few big ones can save you more over time than cutting out a daily latte habit. Here are some of my favorite tactics you can try while on your No-Spend Challenge to increase your household money-saving efforts.

Transportation

For most people, changing the way you get around town is a major inconvenience. But that doesn't mean there's no way you can change small habits to save money.

To save on gas, accelerate gradually to your desired speed and put enough space between you and other cars to keep from braking excessively. Remove anything that makes your car less aerodynamic, like bike and roof racks.

If you can help it, don't let your car sit idle for more than a minute—ideally no more than 30 seconds. In the summer, buy gas at the coolest time of day, early in the morning or at night. The cooler the gas, the denser it is, meaning you'll get more for your buck.

Proper maintenance can save you in the long run, too. Correct tire pressure (checked seasonally), regular oil changes, and fresh filters improve fuel efficiency. If you really want to impact your transportation costs, start biking to work once a week, use public transportation, and skip those expensive car washes.

Housing

Your rent or mortgage should ideally take up less than 25% of your take-home pay. If it's more than that, then you're going to have a tougher time making big payments to your debt or toward your savings account.

If you rent, the easiest way to reduce your housing costs is to get a roommate. If that's not an option, consider moving. Yes, living outside the city for a few years is going to be inconvenient but it's worth it if you'll save a significant amount over the added costs of gas or public transit.

If you own your home, try renting out a room on Airbnb or raising your insurance deductible. If that's still too much, you might want to consider selling and downsizing.

Auto Insurance

When's the last time you negotiated your auto insurance? The average cost for a 30-year-old to insure a car for one year is $2,078. That number varies by a lot of factors, but hopefully, you're on the lower half of that average.

Negotiating and shopping around for your auto insurance policy once a year ensures you're getting the lowest price possible. And I promise it's not that hard.

First off, I don't think you should go with the cheapest policy around just because it's the cheapest. This is one of those cases where buying the premium option may be worth paying a little extra. That said, we go with the cheapest option in our area and it's a widely recognized company.

Electricity, Water & Gas

A lot of utility savings are nickel-and-diming level. But there are some simple habits you can learn to make a long-term difference in your bills.

- Use natural light whenever possible or lamps instead of ceiling lights.
- Keep your shower time to fewer than five minutes.
- Turn off the water when brushing teeth, washing dishes, shaving, etc.
- Unplug electronics while not in use.
- Keep the house slightly chilly in winter, and run the fans in the summer.
- Run full loads of laundry and wash in cold water. Consider air-drying if you have the space.
- Use a crockpot or toaster oven. They keep the house cooler in the summer and use less energy than the oven.

Cable & Streaming Services

You used to be able to say "cut the cord" and help people save money but that's no longer the case. Nowadays, every channel has its own streaming service too. If you're jumping ship and going back to cable, negotiate with your cable provider for a lower rate. Don't be pressured into bundling if it doesn't save you money. If you can't get a lower price, then cut your service back.

Otherwise, choose one streaming service per year. That way you don't miss out forever but you're not paying for eight services at once.

Healthcare

Health insurance is a financial necessity. Healthcare costs are the number-one cause of bankruptcy and can turn the best-laid plans upside down in a second.

If you have it available, take advantage of a Health Savings Account. The contributions are pre-tax and interest on the account grows tax-deferred.

If your employer doesn't cover you, check to see how much you can get in subsidies from the healthcare marketplace. You might also want to consult with a health insurance broker to see if there are better deals for you outside of the marketplace.

Finally, if you're healthy and don't see the inside of a doctor's office except in emergencies, then Healthcare Sharing Ministries are a great low-cost option. These are intended for people of the Christian faith, but you can find more inclusive programs that just require you to agree with certain lifestyle practices like minimal drinking.

Charity

I'm a huge proponent of giving. Too many people think they have to work for low-paying nonprofits to make a difference in the world, but I don't think that's true. If your budget is tight but giving is a priority for you, here are some alternatives:

- Volunteer time at Habitat for Humanity or a local organization
- Donate business clothes to Dress for Success
- Donate formal dresses to Becca's Closet
- Give blood, especially if you're type O or AB
- Crochet a blanket for Project Linus

Don't let the busyness of life keep you from seeing the bigger picture. We're all in this together, whether we have a little or a lot. Practicing generosity now will increase the likeliness you'll give when you have more. And just think what a bunch of millennials without any student loan payments can do to make their community (and the world!) a better place.

Decluttering and Selling Your Stuff

You might be able to tell by now I'm obsessed with the psychology behind why we do the things we don't want to, and vice versa. I'm a sucker for a good scientific study.

There are numerous studies on the way clutter and cleanliness affect our brains and overall health. Long story short: When you walk out the front door, you take your home with you.

A study of the physical activity of 998 Americans showed that those who kept a tidy home were healthier and more active regardless of any other factor. Another study showed women who described their living room as "cluttered" had higher levels of stress-making cortisol (hi again, cortisol!) than women who described their homes as "restful."

The No-Spend Challenge is a time set apart from your regular life full of social engagements and trips. I think it's the best time to start decluttering your house or apartment.

You might think you don't have enough stuff to make an impact, or maybe you watched "The Minimalists" documentary and you're ready to purge all of your belongings. **The emphasis is less on how much you get rid of and more on the act of letting go.**

Less stuff will make your house more tranquil and restful. With less clutter comes less desire to "complete" the look. Not only is it about keeping money in your pocket—if you can sell some of your old stuff, decluttering can be a moneymaker, too. So here is my method for doing both.

Mentally Prepare Mentally & Physically

When purging unused items, it's important to go in knowing what you're up against. The goal isn't to go from hoarder to Ikea showroom in one day. Purging is a process. The reason I love decluttering while on a No-Spend Challenge is that it's unlikely I'll replace the stuff I get rid of during that process.

Also, you have to give up the "I paid $$$ for this" mentality. What you paid for it mattered to your budget (or lack of one) when you bought it. The fact that you're not using it is what matters today. If you haven't used it this year, then you can live without it. You may not be able to make it through your whole house in one challenge so do some things to prepare for future decluttering.

Try this hanger trick, made famous by Oprah: Go into your closet and turn all the hangers the wrong way (whatever that means to you). Whenever you put a garment back into the closet after wearing it, put it in with the hanger facing the right way. At the end of six months or a year, whichever hangers are still facing the wrong way—and the clothing hanging on them—can easily be removed from your closet.

Keep – Sell/Give – Store

When going through drawers and closets that have become a black hole of clutter, find three boxes and label them: keep, sell/give, and store. There could also be a fourth box for trash but I like to keep it simple and just bring the trash can over.

The Keep box is for things you use and still need easy access to. The Sell/Give box gets an attempt at selling, then if that fails, goes to charity; and the Store box is for things you need or want but can go into deep storage.

I also like the Store box as a tester for getting rid of more on my next purge. If you're holding that snow globe from middle school and you're having a hard time parting with it, you don't have to make a decision yet. Put it in the Store box and come back to it in a month.

Don't Call It Junk

When we were hosting a garage sale for my mom, we had a lot of clothes leftover. I went through and tried to separate what we could sell to Plato's Closet, which buys and sells gently used clothes for women.

There were these two pairs of corduroy overalls, one with Eeyore on the front, the other with Pooh and Piglet. Assuming I knew what was in style, I put those in the Give box. But Travis was convinced they would sell. I don't remember everything I said, but it was something to the extent of "You're crazy, these are ugly." But because I wanted to prove him wrong I let him take them.

When we picked up our two bins of clothing at Plato's I was shocked. They'd agreed to buy three items from us. Two of them were the overalls. The lesson: I don't call anything "junk" anymore (well, I'm at least trying now). You might be shocked too at what people will buy online or at second-hand stores.

Find Storage

Don't buy storage. You're trying not to spend money, remember? You don't even know how much storage you're going to need until after you finish. Trust me, I too have dreams about the Container Store, but use it as a reward instead of a solution.

Use what you have available for free first. Wrap boxes with ribbon or washi tape for custom storage or look for free storage on Craigslist and Facebook Marketplace. I try to make it my goal to get rid of enough stuff to eliminate the need for containers.

Wait a few months after finishing the decluttering effort. If it still bothers you, then you can go buy exactly what you need. But chances are, you won't even think about it once it's done.

Work on One Room at a Time

Don't try to tackle the whole house in one day. Not even a month. Two to four hours at a time is about how much most people can handle at a time but I say set a timer and shoot for 30 minutes a day. Start small and tackle one room, closet or drawer at a time and just keep going.

Suggestions for quick purges:
- Old magazines
- Stretched out hair ties
- Unused CDs & DVDs
- Unused makeup and skincare
- Free t-shirts
- Unwanted gifts
- Unused purses

Purge

There are a few ways to go about this. Facebook Marketplace is my go-to starting point to sell anything and OfferUp is my second try. Always sell to the first person who can get it, don't allow hold requests, and accept cash only.

You can also go with a resale store like Plato's Closet for clothes, or Play It Again Sports for sporting equipment. These places typically take a narrow list of items, but it's worth it if you don't have the time to sell everything individually.

Either one is a good option because you're making some dough and you have a clean house! Here are some more ideas on where to sell your stuff and what these services buy:

- Decluttr: Games, CDs, DVDs, books, tech
- Gone: Electronics
- ThredUp: Clothes
- Poshmark: Clothes
- Letgo
- Mercari
- eBay
- Amazon

You could also try a clothing swap party. Everyone brings the clothes they're ready to get rid of and leaves with a few new pieces to add to their wardrobe. You can donate the leftovers or bring them to your local thrift store. Not only did you just have some sweet time with friends; you also decluttered!

An alternative to the clothing swap party is the pantry party. The challenge is to raid your pantry (for some it might not be a challenge) and make a dish to share. You can only use foods you already have—no buying extras! It's a great way to get rid of that box of quinoa you bought when you were trying to be healthy that one time.

Last but not least, try a group yard sale. If you and your friends all have something to sell, then you could end up with a big sale that attracts a lot of buyers. And having more people to advertise for your sale increases your cash-making possibilities.

Tips For Doing Everything All at Once

Don't.

You don't need to do everything at once. This guide is meant to help you through every aspect of a No-Spend Challenge, mentally, emotionally, and physically. But don't feel like you need to do everything in this book to have a successful No-Spend Challenge. By just completing a challenge, you're ahead of people still ignoring their debt.

One of the main themes I hope you'll remember from this book is to keep your focus narrow. It's very hard to achieve a bunch of life changes all at once. Work on one thing until you're (mostly) confident in it, then add something else.

Reaching financial freedom is a marathon, and if you're trying to go from couch to seven-minute mile, you will get discouraged and give up. Don't compare yourself to others, just try to improve yourself.

GO DO THE THINGS:
- **Pick a side hustle and start earning**
- **Negotiate one of your monthly bills down**
- **Clean out a drawer in your house**

8

Beyond the Challenge

The morning after my No-Spend Challenge ends, you can find me at the nice coffee shop getting a fancy latte. Because if I bought a $6 latte every day, I'd feel guilty, but getting one to celebrate a month of not spending feels like a reward.

But after that, it's back to the grind.

I'm all for rewarding yourself after a No-Spend Challenge. But extreme actions can produce an equal and opposite reaction if you're not careful. Don't use your positive accomplishments to justify limiting behavior.

Lots of people pay off their debt only to go right back in or stop spending for a year just to make new limiting spending habits. So what does it take to step out of an extreme season with restraint? The answer is more intentional action, or rather, intentional pausing.

We are busier and more distracted than ever. It's easy to jump from one thing to the next with a false sense of progress just to fall back into old habits and not understand what went awry. It can also be awkward or painful to pause and think about what you did wrong, what could've gone better, and celebrate what went well.

But to get the most out of it, it's essential to pause and reflect during and after every No-Spend Challenge. You need that time to identify what needs more work, funnel saved money to your goals before you spend it, and decide if or when you'll do your next challenge.

Through self-reflection, your self-awareness grows. And the more aware you are of your inner programming, the closer you are to financial freedom that aligns with your core values.

There are two different types of self-reflection. One is a problem- or solution-focused approach where people constructively reflect on how best to reach their goals.

The other is a self-focused approach where individuals attempt to understand or contain their negative emotional and behavioral reactions.

While both are beneficial, problem-focused self-reflection helps more with goal achievement, so this chapter focuses on those techniques.

One tip before you start: Give yourself grace when reflecting. The goal is not to judge your challenge performance, but to reflect on your actions and thoughts, learn from them, and make whatever changes you feel are appropriate for you in the here and now.

Spend Your Money

The first thing you should do after a No-Spend Challenge is to "spend" your saved money on what it was intended to go toward. Hopefully, you decided what you're going to do with your saved money before you started your challenge, but if not, now's the time to do it.

As soon as your challenge is over (or before!), transfer your money to the credit card company, loan servicer, separate savings account, or wherever it's needed to get you closer to your financial goal.

I used to make an extra debt payment the day before my No-Spend Challenge ended so I was still motivated and wouldn't get distracted enough to spend it elsewhere.

If you're saving for something larger, then still remove the money from your spending account to a separate savings account. It's easier to justify spending money you can see. The old wisdom of "out of sight, out of mind" really does work.

Here you'll reflect on both the practice of getting closer to your financial goal and the goal itself.

1. How does it feel to make above-average progress toward your goal?
2. Do you believe you're capable of more now than you did before the challenge?
3. How far are you from your goal? How do you feel about that?
4. Do you feel like your goal is still in alignment with your values?

If you're starting a new month after your No-Spend Challenge, then have your next month's budget done before your challenge ends. If you're mid-month then revisit your budget. Ask yourself how it feels and decide if you want to rework anything. Your new budget shouldn't look like a dramatic change, but a slight improvement.

Many people try to jump straight from mindless spending into calculated moderation. It's easy to make the "perfect" budget but it's near impossible to stick to it. Even after doing a No-Spend Challenge.

Instead of focusing so much on your budget, shift your thinking to work on building better habits. When you've built growth habits, sticking to your budget will be a byproduct and you won't have to think about it as much.

What Needs to Change?

That brings us to our next step: Look back on your experience and go through your spending journal to see what you need to focus on beyond the challenge.

Your goal here is to make a plan to break limiting habits and build growth habits while being free to spend. Because again, once you leave the challenge bubble, it becomes much harder to choose the "right" thing.

Try to focus on one habit at a time. The less you focus on, the more intentional you'll be, and the faster you'll break (or establish) your habit.

Here are some reflection questions to ask yourself:

1. What's the most significant thing you learned from the last [30] days?
2. What's one habit you're going to focus on moving forward as a result of what you learned?
3. What were some of the changes you made to your routine to avoid spending money?
4. What's one change you'll take with you beyond the challenge?
5. What's one change you will not take with you?
6. Did you feel deprived during your challenge?
7. Is there a way you could've creatively met those needs without spending?
8. How much did you save in total?

9. How much discretionary spending will you add back to your budget next month?

Continue to journal about your spending after your No-Spend Challenge. It'll help you decide when to do your next challenge and which expenses to cut out.

Also, changing doesn't just mean spending less. Sometimes it means spending more or differently. Once you've done a few No-Spend Challenges and you've given up bigger items, you'll have a better idea about what you *want* to spend money on.

I gave up Crossfit for nine months on our debt-free journey. For nine months I tried free and cheaper alternatives. I ran, rock-climbed, and did Crossfit-like classes at the YMCA, but it wasn't the same.

I really tried to get creative but nothing motivated me to consistently work out like the structure, variety, and camaraderie of CrossFit. When friends from my old gym bought a new gym, it was the inspiration I needed to go back. I negotiated a deal with them and have been a regular there since.

I am the worst at weightlifting and pretty much everything fitness-related, but my soul and my sanity need that hour per day to be fulfilled. And even with the added expense, we were still able to pay off a crazy amount of debt at the speed of light.

Coming from someone who picked the most expensive type of physical activity to value, I am a firm believer in making room in the budget to fill your soul with what matters to you. Over time your No-Spend Challenges will show you what that is for you.

Now, you can't just decide *everything* matters to you but when you find it, don't feel guilty. The journey is just as important as the destination and sometimes the things we value cost money.

We work for tomorrow, but we aren't promised it. So hold onto what matters.

Once you find what you value, it somehow becomes more valuable. I work out way more than I did before I gave up CrossFit because I'm so thankful to have found it and I know how much I'm paying for it. I don't get burnt out because I know what else is out there and I know it's not for me. But I would've never known that if I hadn't tried.

Maybe yours is art, ultimate Frisbee, or video games. It doesn't matter how ridiculous other people think it is. Let the haters judge, because in the end, they'll still be complaining and you will have financial freedom.

Look Toward Your Next Challenge

Depending on how much debt you have to pay off and the income you have to pay it, you may want to jump right into your next challenge or space them out as regular "cleanses." By now, you know that not spending is hard, and there's a reason people call it a No-Spend *Challenge*.

The crazy thing is, a No-Spend Challenge will probably feel easier than sticking to a budget. It's much easier to say "no" to everything than it is to decide what's worth your money and what's not. Decision fatigue is real so be careful when re-entering society after the challenge.

Continue to practice the money-saving tactics you just read, and prepare for your next challenge by working on the growth habits you just laid out.

Reflect now on how you'll look forward to your next challenge and how you'll change things next time.

1. Do you think you need to do another No-Spend Challenge? Why or why not?
2. If yes, when will your next challenge be?
3. How will you look forward to your next challenge while spending regularly?
4. How do you want to up your game for next time?
5. Will you go any longer?
6. How will you give up more or differently?
7. How will you spend your time differently? For example, will you side hustle or declutter more?

Challenging yourself is how you get better. No one's perfect their first time attempting a No-Spend Challenge. Keep pushing yourself, and eventually, you'll achieve frugality.

It's a good idea to plan your future challenges around any weekend getaways, anniversaries, or birthdays. Don't wait until the last minute and remember you have a fun event during a challenge. Remember that you can always make it work as an exception but if you can plan, why wouldn't you?

Also, remember that the break between challenges isn't about being able to spend money. It's about taking time to enjoy the journey.

If you're anything like me, sometimes you minimize your accomplishments because you feel like you're still playing catch-up. You may feel like you need to do a bunch of No-Spend Challenges or even a year to speed things up. Wherever you're at, you're not behind. Enjoying the journey and making tough budgeting decisions teaches you just as much as a challenge.

Your Turn

It's unlikely your life will change completely after one No-Spend Challenge. But it's very likely a few things will start to transform. And every time you do a No-Spend Challenge, you'll be able to go longer, give up more, and get through it more easily.

You'll learn to simplify your life and get more creative. To cut out things that aren't valuable and elevate the things that are. They weren't lying when they said the best things in life are free. And the less you spend, the more you'll see that.

Someone recently told me it's "outside the reality spectrum" for most people to pay off massive amounts of debt in a short time, due to low income and the normal cost of living. I agree. If your income is low and you maintain a "normal" cost of living, you will not be able to pay off your debt quickly, if at all.

But if you've made it this far, you've decided you don't want to be normal.

You can do this. Whether it takes you two years or seven, you can do it. And it's a short season in the scope of things, even if it feels like a lifetime. After four years of being consumer debt-free, I'm now focused on investing and growing a business where my goals are taking much longer than paying off debt did.

It's hard to see the light when you're deep in the middle of the tunnel but know that it's there. I hope this is a guide you read and reread to improve yourself and your spending habits along the journey. I hope that if you've felt like you're just spinning your wheels, this guide helps you move the needle on your financial goals.

GO DO THE THINGS:
- **Get closer to your goal**
- **Make a plan to change one thing**
- **Look forward to what's next**

9

Need More Support?

When I was on my debt payoff journey I felt like I was on an island. Even now being financially responsible is still counter to the way many people around us live their lives.

Financial freedom is amazing and I'd still take this feeling of being a weird outsider over the burden my debt and overspending put on me.

Lucky for you, you don't have to do this alone.

If one book and one new skill aren't enough and you feel like you need more support my Frugal Friends co-host Jill and I have created the Financial Freedom Mentorship. It brings together everything we know to be most important on your journey to your first $100,000 in net worth: education, action, and community.

Education: The program starts with our Financial Freedom Simplified course that covers the basics of values-aligned financial goals, frugal living, increasing your income, investing, and more. If there's anything you need to know to reach financial freedom, it's covered in this course. You'll also get access to every guest expert Q&A we've brought into the program.

Action: You'll have the opportunity to act on what you've learned by doing 30-day challenges with other mentees. Challenges range from meal planning and minimalism to side hustling and investing for retirement. You'll also have the opportunity to speak to me and Jill directly at our group mentoring calls twice a month. We'll answer your questions and bring in guest experts to speak on specialized topics.

Community: Last, but arguably most importantly, you'll be immersed in an active community of other women who are saving money, getting out of debt, and working on building their $100K net worth. You'll have the opportunity to create accountability groups and do challenges with other mentees. Our community server allows you to do video calls with your group within the platform as well as topical chats on many popular finance topics.

We created the Financial Freedom Mentorship as a way to invest in your success but in a group setting that allows for collaboration and a more affordable price point! If you don't have people in your life who are encouraging you and working alongside you to reach similar goals, this Mentorship was made for you.

Learn more about the Financial Freedom Mentorship and join us for our next group call at www.ModernFrugality.com/FFM We can't wait to start supporting you further.

Made in the USA
Columbia, SC
16 January 2025

51989643R00074